AN HOLISTIC APPROACH TO PHYSICAL EDUCATION CURRICULA: OBJECTIVES CLASSIFICATION SYSTEM FOR ELEMENTARY SCHOOLS by

Margaret M. Thompson, Ph.D.
and
Professor of Physical Education
University of Illinois, Urbana-Champaign

Barbara A. Mann, M.S.
Lecturer, Division of Child Development
Lecturer, Department of Physical Education
University of Illinois, Urbana-Champaign

ISBN 0-87563-131-2

Published by
STIPES PUBLISHING COMPANY
10-12 Chester Street
Champaign, Illinois 61820

A note of thanks to the many people

who have helped us in many ways

. . . .

This book is dedicated to them, and to

MADELINE SHAWEN THOMPSON

AND

MARGUERITE ALBERT MANN

1. Physical education for children
2. Physical education (Elementary)

I. Mann, Barbara A
II. Title

Preface

We believe that elementary physical education as it is known today must change drastically to benefit children and coincide with the educational mainstream. It is our hope that the classification system presented may be used directly or indirectly toward those ends. This book is offered with the intent of advancing usable concepts in the development of children's physical education programs.

The book is arranged first with the historical background to help those students concerned with further taxonomic developments. The Thompson-Mann taxonomy is next presented without explanation to serve the reader as a quick referent to the needs of the child in program development. The taxonomy explanation follows to serve as content resource for construction of behavioral objectives. Chapter four deals with the application of the taxonomy and positions for curricular change. The curriculum development of chapter five explains step-wise progression in curriculum construction. Chapters six, seven, eight and nine relate the experiences of the authors and the Hazelwood School District representatives in construction of the Hazelwood elementary schools physical education curriculum. Appendix A, B, and C are examples of taxonomy utilization for a specific age group youngster (five to seven years of age).

The compilation of this book has led us to ongoing taxonomic based curricular development at Holy Cross Elementary School (Champaign, Ill.) where component analyses and content validation of the physical education program are being studied. We look forward to sharing those results in a future publication. The reflections of readers are eagerly sought, welcome, and will be considered for future study and publication direction.

Margaret M. Thompson
Professor of Physical Education
University of Illinois
Urbana-Champaign

Barbara A. Mann
Lecturer, Division of Child
    Development
Lecturer, Department of
    Physical Education
University of Illinois
Urbana-Champaign

Table of Contents

PREFACE iii

CHAPTER ONE:

History and Development of the Taxonomy for Physical
Education 1

CHAPTER TWO:

Physical Education Taxonomy 3

CHAPTER THREE:

Explanation of the Taxonomic Categories 9

CHAPTER FOUR:

Application of the Taxonomy 27

CHAPTER FIVE:

Curriculum Development 31

CHAPTER SIX:

Development of the Hazelwood Curriculum 37

CHAPTER SEVEN:

Behavioral Expectations by Category 41

CHAPTER EIGHT:

Hazelwood Behavioral Objectives and Learning Experiences . 71

CHAPTER NINE:

Hazelwood Charts 139

BIBLIOGRAPHY 153

APPENDIX 155

   A: Sample Objectives and Experiences 156

   B: Planning Daily Lessons 172

   C: Sample Daily Lessons 175

Chapter One
History and Development of the Taxonomy
for Physical Education

Educational objectives serve as guides for the establishment of competency based learning programs. This was voiced at the AAHPER National Conference on Professional Preparation (1974), and the AOTE National Conference on Redesigning Teacher Education (1973). However, the clarity of psychomotor educational objectives has not yet been established and thus competency based programs are floundering without supportive direction.

Determination of educational goals relevant to the developmental levels of the learners is one of the most important criteria in curriculum design. Among the most significant guidelines for the development of educational goals are those developed for the cognitive domain by Bloom (1956), and for the affective domain by Krathwohl, et. al. (1964). The group of college examiners attending the 1948 American Psychological Association Convention who conceived the idea of a classification system of educational goals, recognized the existence of the psychomotor domain, but made no preparation for developing a classification system.

As concern for the development of curricula in elementary and secondary schools which would provide more meaningful education for all children increased, physical educators and some educators began to consider the idea of developing a classification system for educational goals in the psychomotor domain. Simpson (1966), Clein and Stone (1970), Jewett, et. al. (1971), Harrow (1972), and the U.C.L.A. Instructional Objectives Exchange (circa 1969), are among those contributing to the formulation of psychomotor taxonomies. Despite the worthwhile attempts of Bloom, Krathwohl, and those concerned with the psychomotor domain, it appears paradoxical to separate educational goals into three classifications when the unity or wholeness of man is constantly being emphasized.

An attempt at unifying the individual domains into a classification system for physical education objectives was made by Thompson in 1969. This system was a simple arrangement of five categories of development, (mental, social-emotional, physical, body handling, and object handling) to which physical education objectives could be assigned. These categories were utilized by Gordon (1971), and by Gordon, Thompson, and Alspaugh (1973) for ranking the importance of behavioral objectives in physical education for children in kindergarten through grade two.

The major weakness of this classification system was that it did not provide sub-categories which would assist the writer of objectives in the determination of adequate coverage within a major category. Experimentation with the use of the taxonomy began in 1972-73 at the Holy Cross Elementary School in Champaign, Illinois

(Thompson, Mann, and Dewhirst, 1973), and a detailed classification system (taxonomy) was produced for the writing of behavioral objectives in physical education. The resultant taxonomy contained elements of the Bloom (1956) and Krathwohl (1964) taxonomies, as well as the five categories used by Gordon in 1971, with an additional category termed Coordinated Body and Object Handling. Sub-categories were delineated for each major category.

Further experimentation at Holy Cross Elementary School involved the development of behavioral objectives for each grade level and the selection of learning experiences by which objectives could be attained by the learners in grades K through seven.

Additional use of this taxonomy for curriculum development was initiated in the Hazelwood School District, St. Louis County, Missouri, during the 1974-75 school year. Thompson and Mann met with a task force of ten physical educators, representing nineteen elementary schools, and their physical education coordinator, (Roy Tanner), to formulate behavioral objectives and learning experiences based on the taxonomy for children in grades K through six. the objectives and their corresponding learning experiences were then organized into a yearly curriculum per grade level. Formulation of the objectives was based on a set of behavioral expectations designed by Mann and Thompson.

Construction of the classification system and the determination of its application were influenced by insights gained in working with pre-school children at the University of Missouri-Columbia, the University of Missouri-St. Louis, and the University of Illinois, Urbana-Champaign. Further evidence of the need for integrating all aspects of development was noted during the designing of curricula for Holy Cross Elementary School and the Hazelwood School District. The resultant taxonomy reflects the authors' concerns for providing a classification system, based on an holistic development of children, which would enable teachers to design curricula directed toward this concept.

2

Chapter Two
Physical Education Taxonomy

1.0 Mental Development

    1.10   Knowledges and Understandings of the Human Body

        1.11 Body parts and body segments
        1.12 Differentation among body parts and segments

    1.20   Knowledges and Understandings of Movement Patterns and Skills

        1.21 Patterns and skills terminology
        1.22 Purpose and use of skills
        1.23 Pattern and skill continuity

    1.30   Knowledges and Understandings of Mechanical Principles of Movement

        1.31 Locomotion
        1.32 Body Parts
        1.33 Propulsion of objects
        1.34 Receipt of objects

    1.40   Knowledges and Understandings of Physiologic Factors

        1.41 Factors important to human movement
        1.42 Physiologic functioning and physical activity
        1.43 Factors of physical fitness

    1.50   Knowledges and Understanding of Rules and Strategies

        1.51 Rules and/or performance regulations for specific activities
        1.52 Strategies for specific activities
        1.53 Safety factors related to rules and strategies

    1.60   Knowledges and Understandings of Common/Related Concepts

        1.61 Art
        1.62 Language Arts
        1.63 Mathematics
        1.64 Music
        1.65 Science
        1.66 Social Science

2.0 Social-Emotional Development

    2.10   Appreciation and Acceptance of Physical Activity

2.11   Enjoyment in physical endeavor
2.12   Effects of physical activity
2.13   Participation in movement activities
2.14   Achievement of skill and success in movement activities
2.15   Non-verbal communication through movement

2.20   Values of Positive Self-concept

     2.21   Abilities and limitations
     2.22   Body image
     2.23   Self-discipline
     2.24   Self-direction

2.30   Values Relating to Others

     2.31   Competition
     2.32   Cooperation
     2.33   Abilities and limitations of others
     2.34   Values and value systems of others
     2.35   Behavior of others

2.40   Concepts Regarding Groups

     2.41   Variety in group structures
     2.42   Work in variety of groups

          2.421   Decision making
          2.422   Contribution
          2.423   Identification

2.50   Values Related to The Development of Humor and Empathy

     2.51   Incongruent behavior in self and others
     2.52   Incongruity potential
     2.53   Incongruity assignment appropriateness

3.0   Physical Development

  3.10   Agility

     3.11   Stop and Start
     3.12   Change direction
     3.13   Change levels

  3.20   Balance

     3.21   Static
     3.22   Dynamic

  3.30   Coordination

     3.31   Eye-hand
     3.32   Eye-foot
     3.33   Speed

3.40   Endurance

    3.41   Cardiovascular
    3.42   Muscular

3.50   Flexibility

    3.51   Neck
    3.52   Trunk
    3.53   Limbs
    3.54   Extremities

3.60   Kinesthesis

    3.61   Non-locomotor and locomotor tasks
    3.62   Object handling tasks
    3.63   Varying environments

3.70   Rhythm

    3.71   Self imposed
    3.72   Externally imposed

3.80   Strength

    3.81   Arm strength
    3.82   Leg strength
    3.83   Total body strength

3.90   Power

    3.91   Arm power
    3.92   Leg power

4.0   Body Handling Development

4.10   Sensori-motor Abilities

    4.11   Body Awareness
    4.12   Body in relation to space
    4.13   Body in relation to surrounding objects
    4.14   Discrimination

        4.141   Auditory
        4.142   Visual
        4.143   Tactile
        4.144   Kinesthetic

4.20   Non-locomotor Patterns and Skills

    4.21   Total body
    4.22   Body parts and segments

4.30   Locomotor Patterns and Skills

4.31 Propulsion
4.32 Absorption

4.40 Combining Locomotor and Non-locomotor Patterns and Skills

    4.41 Arm Movements
    4.42 Segmental Movements

4.50 Combining Locomotor, Non-locomotor and Body Awareness

    4.51 Laterality
    4.52 Balance

4.60 Movement Communication

    4.61 Imitative
    4.62 Expressive
    4.63 Interpretative

5.0 Object Handling Development

5.10 Sensori-motor Abilities

    5.11 Visual discrimination
    5.12 Auditory discrimination
    5.13 Tactile discrimination
    5.14 Kinesthetic discrimination

5.20 Coordination

    5.21 Eye-hand
    5.22 Eye-foot

5.30 Propulsion

    5.31 Accuracy
    5.32 Distance
    5.33 Speed

5.40 Absorption

    5.41 Hand
    5.42 Implement in hand

6.0 Coordinated Body and Object Handling Development

6.10 Coordination

    6.11 Eye-hand-locomotion
    6.12 Eye-foot-locomotion

6.20 Propulsion of objects-locomotion

    6.21 Accuracy
    6.22 Distance
    6.23 Speed

6.30 Object Absorption-locomotion

      6.31 Control of body weight
      6.32 Control of object force

Chapter Three
Explanation of the Taxonomic Categories

1.0 MENTAL DEVELOPMENT

The Mental Development category is concerned with the acquisition of those knowledges and understandings pertinent to the how and why of body functioning, as it is controlled by human form and as it is the precursor of form. Also, the root of cognition is in the sensory enaction with the unknown. The generalizations which may occur as a result of physiological function and the result of practice experience are determined by the individual's genetic propensity and the environmental influences upon him.

The reader is reminded that this mental development category is formulated as a structural component referent for physical education curricula development. It does not serve as an exemplary categorization of human mental development, but rather incorporates previous taxonomic works toward specialized program development. Mental development cannot be isolated from any of the five other categories for the purpose of designing program.

1.10 Knowledges and Understandings of the Human Body

Recognition, identification, and differentiation of the body and its parts and segments are a direct result of performance experience. The identification of specific parts, segments, and concepts of laterality are reflections of performance generalizations.

  1.11 Body parts and body segments: Recognition and identification of specific body parts (nose, fingers, legs, etc.) and segments (head, trunk, neck, etc.).

  1.12 Differentiation among body parts and segments: Concepts of laterality and relationship of specific part(s) to total body (front, back, right and left sides, top, bottom).

1.20 Knowledges and Understandings of Movement Patterns and Skills.

The term movement pattern refers to observable fundamental purposeful motor acts representing integration of generalized body movements with segregated reflex movements into an integrated whole. Movement skills refers to those observable motor acts which involve modification of a movement pattern or combination of movement patterns for a movement purpose stressing precision and/or accuracy. A run in which the concern is for presence of the basic elements of the run and for rapid locomotion from one place to another would be classified as a running pattern. A run in which the concern is modified to include length of stride, degree of arm movement, degree of body lean to achieve sprinting-type speed equates to running as a skill. The difference between a skill and a movement pattern can also be illustrated by comparing the purpose of the performance. The purpose of the movement pattern is simply the performance of that movement pattern, whereas the purpose of a skill act is concerned with acquisition of some external goal (Godfrey, Thompson 1966).*

    1.21   <u>Patterns and skills terminology</u>: Recognition, identification, and differentiation among the various body handling and object handling patterns and skills. Ability to perform the various patterns and skills is included in taxonomic categories 3.0, 4.0, 5.0, and 6.0.

    1.22   <u>Purpose and use of skills</u>: Inclusion of what can be accomplished by a skill, when to use a particular skill, and how to use it in specific situations. This infers adaptations in aspects of the preparatory, execution, and termination phases of the skill, as well as selection of the most desirable skill to achieve the task. For example, the selection of an overhand throw when the desired end is to achieve distance.

    1.23   <u>Pattern and skill continuity</u>: Includes continuity from generalization to specificity in patterns, from pattern specificity to skill specificity, from skill specificity to purposeful integrated performance (generalization) which is made possible through plasticity among aspects of the preparatory, execution, and termination phases of the behavior, as well as performance variations stemming from the continuity phenomenon. Timing is a basic consideration in this process.

1.30   <u>Knowledges and Understandings of Mechanical Principles of Movement</u>.

    1.31   <u>Locomotion</u>: Laws of motion applied to moving the body in, on, and through land, air, and water environments. Functions of balance, gravity, buoyancy, resistance, propulsion, and absorption of body force, etc. on locomotion are considered.

    1.32   <u>Body parts</u>: Influence of body parts on total body and other body parts in performance of body handling and object handling patterns and skills. Consideration is also given to leverage, action-reaction, changes in center of gravity, transfer of momentum and summation of forces.

---

*The entire 1.20 category stems from writings and lectures of and professional discussions between Thompson and Godfrey during the period 1958-1970.

1.33 <u>Propulsion of objects</u>: Consideration of air resistance, angle of impact and release, characteristics of object propelled, flow, force, timing, gravity, leverage, transfer of momentum, translatory and rotatory motion, etc. as they influence effectiveness of propulsive object handling.

1.34 <u>Receipt of objects</u>: Consideration of object characteristics such as size, weight, mass, texture, oncoming force of object as they influence the effectiveness of the absorptive patterns of object handling. Also considered are principles for controlled absorption such as increase of surface areas, distance, and time to reduce velocity of the oncoming object.

1.40 <u>Knowledges and Understandings of Physiologic Factors</u>.

1.41 <u>Factors important to human movement</u>: Roles of nutrition, health status, fatigue, emotional stress, and relaxation in performance. Additional influences of age, weight, body type, sex, and genetic propensity are included.

1.42 <u>Physiologic functioning and physical activity</u>: Consideration of reaction time, response time, movement time, reflex time, perception, selectivity of cueing, inhibition, feedback, retention, transfer, mental and physical practice. Also includes effects of physical activity on cardio-vascular system, general muscle tone, and total body functioning.

1.43 <u>Factors of physical fitness</u>: Identification of the elements of physical fitness, how to achieve physical fitness, physical fitness as a facilitator of performance in movement activities, and as a defense against environmental stress.

1.50 <u>Knowledges and Understandings of Rules and Strategies</u>:

1.51 <u>Rules and/or performance regulations for specific activities</u>: Limitations specific to simple or complex movement situations involving self or others. Consideration of performance requisites and, where appropriate, considerations for formations and group organizations.

1.52 <u>Strategies for specific activities</u>: Plans of action for the most efficient and effective attainment of the goal of an activity in movement situations involving self or others.

1.53 <u>Safety factors related to rules and strategies</u>: Recognition and identification of potential hazards relative to activity in pursuit; rules as implements of safety.

1.60 Knowledges and Understandings of Common/Related Concepts.

The subheadings in this category encompass concepts from each
of the elementary school curricular areas which are common to
that area and to physical education, and can be planned and
initiated in either area and reinforced by the other. Also
included are concepts which are rather specific to the subject
area and can be meaningfully reinforced through physical education.

    1.61 Art: Recognition, identification, and interpolation of
          concepts regarding shape, form, color, intensity, depth,
          tone consonance, disonance, motion and flow. Considera-
          tion of art as a movement structure and expression
          (symbolic, descriptive, interpretive).

    1.62 Language Arts: Concepts regarding movement as a non-
          literal communication form expanded toward recognition
          and utilization of symbolic language codes (semantics
          and syntax). Understanding that flow of movement forms
          parallels fluidity in speech and literature.

    1.63 Mathematics: Concepts regarding movement as a non-
          literal form expanded toward recognition and utilization
          of symbolic codes (quantitative and qualitative con-
          structs of time, space, and distance). Experiential
          reference elicited by movement performance in constructs.

    1.64 Music: Recognition, identification, interpolation of
          concepts regarding tone, quality, depth, consonance,
          disonance, rhythm, motion, flow, and form. Music as a
          movement structure and expression (symbolic, descrip-
          tive, interpretive) is also included.

    1.65 Science: Recognition, identification, interpretation of
          the organization and structure of physical properties of
          matter and the physical laws of nature are included as
          well as experiential reference elicited by movement per-
          formance.

    1.66 Social Science: Understanding of self, to the expansion
          of understanding of self to others through movement and
          environmental demands; comprehension of functions of
          independence and dependence, cooperation and competition,
          parallelism of demands in forms of governance and demands
          in sports performance (simple to complex).

2.0 SOCIAL-EMOTIONAL DEVELOPMENT

The Social-Emotional Development category includes recognition,
appreciation, and acceptance of values and value systems. Aspects
of Krathwohl's Taxonomy for the Affective Domain (1964) have been
incorporated into this category. The sub-headings utilized in the
Social-Emotional Development Category are directed toward those values and value systems which are inherent in meaningful and satisfying

participation in movement activities. Many of these values are transferable and important in eliciting the formation of value systems for living.

2.10 <u>Appreciation and Acceptance of Physical Activity</u>.

    2.11 <u>Enjoyment in Physical Endeavor</u>: Positive attitudes and pleasure derived from observation and participation in movement activities from fundamental patterns of walking, running, etc., to bicycling, swimming, dancing and complex sports.

    2.12 <u>Effects of Physical Activity</u>: Positive attitudes toward beneficial effects of physical activity such as physiological effects, avenues to socialization, avenues to release of emotional tensions, opportunities for self-expression and self-realization.

    2.13 <u>Participation in Movement Activities</u>: Willingness to participate in movement activities to derive physiologic benefits, pleasure, socialization and creative expression.

    2.14 <u>Achievement of Skill and Success in Movement Activities</u>: Acceptance of desirability of achieving skill and success in movement activities and to establish levels of aspiration within a realistic scope.

    2.15 <u>Non-verbal Communication Through Movement</u>: Recognition of movement as a form of communication and realization of the effects of one's own movement on others. Identification of movements that are expressive; utilization of movement to express a feeling or idea through creative or aesthetic interpretive movement from simple gestures and postures to sophisticated choreography in floor exercise, dance and swimming.

2.20 <u>Values of Positive Self-Concept</u>.

Realization of self yields to self concept; the polarity of the concept reflects the attitudes of the environmental milieu. The favorable or unfavorable assignment of self-concept results as an interaction process of innate tendencies of any individual to and from his reflective population.

    2.21 <u>Abilities and Limitations</u>: Realization of the extent of self and parameters and one's own movement behavior; recognition of own movement capabilities and limitations; willingness to examine them and acceptance of them in light of one's own developmental level; willingness to make growth adjustments where indicated.

    2.22 <u>Body Image</u>: Awareness of self-structure through physical experience and comparative experience with age mates and non-age mates as a determinant of one's potential. Includes concepts of one's own structure in relationship to one's movement capabilities as well as concepts with regard to how others view him.

2.23 **Self-Discipline**: Evaluation from extrinsic to intrinsic conduct values; recognition and acceptance toward realizing responsibility for one's own behavior and a willingness to assume this responsibility.

2.24 **Self-Direction**: The recognition of and motivation toward congruent and socially accepted individual goals.

2.30 **Values Relating to Others.**

Nurturance to survive is no less important than the nurturance of a value structure. The immediate environment of the child allows his active participation in his development of values. Moral judgment is relative to humanity, not individual isolation. The incorporation of the environment reflects growth structure and it is through the child's consideration of few that he becomes capable of consideration of the many.

2.31 **Competition**: Learner evaluation of increments in own performance and in comparison to peer performance; as well as variation in goal setting relative to self and peer comparative experience. To understand the child in conflict with self or others toward any goal is to realize competition as an innate enterprise of development. The conflict change, the number of people he considers in his motivation problem and his goal are processes of life's stages. (The reader is referred to E. H. Erikson, Psychological Issues (Monograph) 1959, for an understanding of conflict stages of life.)

2.32 **Cooperation**: Cooperative enterprise toward self achievement and toward group achievement. Cooperation must be promoted in a planned environment. Through the manipulation of the innate conflicts of competition, promotion of cooperation can be achieved. Beyond the goals of survival, cooperation is a humanistic enterprise, foreign to the nature of the child. Manifestations of cooperation are first seen as a realization of egocentrism. The utilization of group enterprise first dawns as a goal tool for self-satisfaction.

2.33 **Abilities and Limitations of Others**: Realization of the uniqueness of the abilities and limitations of others as well as comparison of own abilities with peers. The subleties of assigned values increase with the child's vision and generalization experience. In his experience with his observations, he relegates not only his own limits and concepts of self abilities, but assigns the classifications and seriations of abilities and limitations of all others.

2.34 Values and Value Systems of Others: Realization of the
     uniqueness of the values and value systems of others,
     as well as comparison of own values and value systems
     with peers. Acceptance or rejection of peer values and
     values of adults is greatly influenced by the degree of
     congruence with the familial model. In the development
     of the child's values, initial dependency is from his
     primal familial model. The child is first of all,
     amoral, having neither positive or negative value desig-
     nations. In other regards, this system development
     parallels the development of 2.33.

2.35 Behavior of Others: Regard for the behavior of others
     as a guide to personal and peer behavior; realization
     of self behavior as an activator and model for peer
     behavior. One individual's behavior towards another
     elicits a response unique to that stimulus. The manner
     with which the child sympathetically or antagonistically
     views the behaviors of others is an interactive result
     of one's own self-concept, level of competition and
     cooperation, acceptance of abilities, limitations, as
     well as values and value systems of others. Thus, the
     behavior of others is also a reflective result of the
     other's behaviors.

2.40 Concepts Regarding Groups.

The child considers himself, than another, then a few and an
even larger number of peers in the stage development model.
The egocentrism of the child limits and promotes his social
adaptivity. Expansion of relations with others is a product
of environmental experience. The key family enclosure and
interaction of individuals and groups into and with the family
determines the child's propensities toward individual expressions of socialization. The size of the family is not as
important as the involvement of the family members with the
community at large.

2.41 Variety in Group Structures: Consideration for members
     of varying group sizes as well as for the benefits de-
     rived from working with groups. Generalizations from
     the known establish the child's confidence to adapt new
     encounters. The child responds to individuals and
     groups with whom he can identify. The trust quality
     necessary for the socialization process stems from the
     family and is further generated from the dyadic, triadic,
     etc. small group encounters of the child.

2.42 Work in Variety of Groups: Consideration of self through
     observation of others in play changes to inclusion of
     self in another's play with extension and evolution of
     goal structure.

     2.421 Decision Making: The planned environment stimu-
           lates the recognition of and communication of

alternatives. Nonacceptance of alternative <u>may be</u> lack of recognition of alternative. The task of recognizing an alternative is not suited to the infant but the infant's realization of goal allows distinction of alternatives. The necessity for decision arises in alternative or multi-alternative situations.

2.422 <u>Contribution</u>: In the early stage of cooperative or organized group participation, there are usually one or two leaders directing the activity. Other members, by role assumption, contribute to success of the objective which has influenced the organization of the group. Thus, group participation can be both perpetrated or incidental as in an interactive model.

A

2.423 <u>Identification</u>: Identification with a group is based on feelings toward group members, commonalities of interests, energy, aptitudes, and peer and adult acceptance. The objective of the group's activity influences the selection of group members.

2.50 <u>Values Related to the Development of Humor and Empathy</u>.

Humor is the realization of the incongrous or absurd performance or events in relation to self and/or others. Achievement of compassion and eventually empathy stem from the awareness and classifications of incongruities. Absurdities or incongruencies which reflect peril, pain, or sadness are realized by experience not to be humorous. Role playing holds major promise for the development of empathy in children.

2.51 <u>Incongruent Behavior in Self and Others</u>: Awareness and sensitivity to incongrous behavior of self and others.

2.52 <u>Incongruity Potential</u>: Awareness of the potential for danger, harm, and derision in incongruity.

2.53 <u>Incongruity Assignment Appropriateness</u>: Awareness of the appropriate assignment of humor/compassion for incongrous behavior.

3.0 PHYSICAL DEVELOPMENT

The Physical Development category encompasses those components necessary to that which is often labeled physical fitness. The items included in physical fitness are agility, balance, coordination, endurance, flexibility, kinesthesis, power, speed and strength. Recognition of the component of rhythm development as noted by Keogh (1968) and Arnett and Thompson (1970) coupled with the authors' conviction of the importance of rhythm to total physical development led to the inclusion of rhythm development as a component in this category. Physical development proceeds from head to tail, center to periphery, and manifests itself from large to small neuro-muscular control in simple to complex tasks as a result of nature and nurturance. Practice, experience, and involvement dictates the degree and extent of performance.

3.10 Agility.

It is defined here as the ability to initiate movement with speed and to continue that movement in a controlled manner under a variety of demands such as quick directional and/or level (high, medium, low) changes, as well as the ability to initiate and terminate movement quickly. It is dependent upon balance, coordination, flexibility, kinesthesis, rhythm, and to a certain extent strength and endurance.

3.11 Stop and Start: The ability to initiate movement and/or to terminate movement quickly without loss of balance or control.

3.12 Change Direction: The ability to execute in a controlled manner rapid directional changes from forward to either side or to reverse direction.

3.13 Change Levels: The ability to execute in a controlled manner rapid change of total body location from high level to low level, low level to middle level, etc.

3.20 Balance.

The ability to resist forces of gravity and other external forces both from the so-called static or stationary postures and from the postures during performance of various locomotor activities is included in this component. It is a condition of equilibrium or the tendency to resist or overcome displacement. Inherent in balance are vision, kinesthetic sense, and minimal levels of strength and endurance.

3.21 Static Balance: The ability to maintain the center of gravity over the base of support in standing, sitting, squatting, with or without movement of body segments or limbs and with purposeful movement of body segments or parts as in twisting, rotating, swinging, etc.

3.22 Dynamic Balance: The ability to react to changes of the center of gravity relationship to the base of support during locomotion (walk, run, etc.) in such a manner that displacement of one or more body parts or segments required for the locomotion task is compensated accordingly by positioning of other parts or segments sufficiently to avoid falling, tripping, etc.

3.30 Coordination.

As defined in the physical development category, coordination refers to the ability to coordinate visual or sensory interpretation in ongoing activity with control of the body or control of an object by the body or a body part. The elements of reaction-response time and sequence of timing are important aspects of both eye-hand and eye-foot coordination. (For variations, see 5.20 and 6.10).

3.31 Eye-Hand Coordination: The ability to coordinate the visually or sensorially perceived movements of the hand(s) to insure control of the body or of the object.

3.32 Eye-Foot Coordination: The ability to coordinate the visually or sensorially perceived movements of the feet to insure control of the body or of the object.

3.33 Speed: The component of performance that accounts for the time that occurs between the initiation of a stimulus and the initiation of the response coupled with the sequence of timing of movements of the body parts to termination of the movements.

3.40 Endurance.

The ability to maintain work efficiency over a time performance. Cardio-vascular functioning and the work capacity of the individual are intricately interwoven. An individual's structural form and the function of the task preclude individual efficiency in muscular developmental performance.

3.41 Cardiovascular Endurance: The capacity of the circulatory system to function during activities which require sustained effort. Status and change in blood pressure and heart rate are the usual indicators of cardiovascular endurance for measurement by physical educators.

3.42 Muscular Endurance: The ability of the individual to handle his own body weight in varying intensity work periods over durations of time. VanHuss and Heusner (1970) describe dynamic muscular endurance in three classifications on a continuum from tasks requiring high intensity work of short endurance such as chin-ups, sit-ups, push-ups, dashes, sprints, to tasks of low intensity work of long duration such as distance cycling, running and swimming.

3.50 Flexibility.

The ability to exhibit range of joint motion toward optimal efficiency within individual structural limits with consideration of protagonists and antagonistic musculature and innervation.

3.51 Neck: As dictated by 3.50 with reference to the neck.

3.52 Trunk: As dictated by 3.50 with reference to the trunk.

3.53 <u>Limbs</u>: As dictated by 3.50 with reference to the arms and legs.

3.54 <u>Extremities</u>: Digital manipulative efficiency (dexterity) as dictated by 3.50.

3.60 <u>Kinesthesis</u>.

The ability to exhibit specific knowledge and awareness of position of the body and body parts placement in and through space (land, water, free space).

3.61 <u>Non-locomotor and locomotor tasks</u>: Awareness of and response to the position of body parts and the body in the performance of locomotor and non-locomotor tasks.

3.62 <u>Object handling tasks</u>: Awareness of and response to position of body parts and the body in the performance of object handling tasks.

3.63 <u>Varying environments</u>: Awareness of and response to position of body parts and the body when on land, in free space, in the water, on snow and on ice.

3.70 <u>Rhythm</u>.

The ability to interpolate or reiterate syncopation. The marking of events in calculation with the rest and pause of relaxation. Relaxation is considered a planned reduction of stimuli to sharpen interpolative referents (giving greater meaning to the environment).

3.71 <u>Self-Imposed</u>: Fluidity and continuity of movement in relation to one's own structure and inner rhythmic sense. The syncopation is individually established, maintained and promoted.

3.72 <u>Externally Imposed</u>: Adaptation of an individual's inner rhythm to the syncopation of the environment.

3.80 <u>Strength</u>.

The capacity of the musculo-skeletal system in meeting the demands of joint/body position stability for a variety of tasks. Strength is a key element in the initiation and facilitation of movement functions. The reverse of strength must be sufficient to meet daily tasks and to cope with survival requirements.

3.81 <u>Arm strength</u>: The ability to support, to lift, and to propel one's own body weight with the arms to meet daily living and survival requirements.

3.82 <u>Leg strength</u>: The ability to support and propel one's own body with the legs to meet daily living and survival requirements.

3.83 <u>Total body strength</u>: The capacity of the body to meet daily living tasks and survival requirements for strength.

3.90 <u>Power</u>.

The ability to exhibit explosive strength with emphasis on speed and timing.

3.91 <u>Arm power</u>: The ability to combine speed and strength of arm movements in explosive propulsion of one's own body and of objects.

3.92 <u>Leg power</u>: The ability to combine speed and strength of leg movements in explosive propulsion of one's own body and of objects.

4.0   BODY HANDLING DEVELOPMENT

The category of Body Handling Development includes the non-locomotor patterns and skills, the locomotor patterns and skills, and their sensori-motor requisites (abilities). The non-locomotor patterns and the locomotor patterns represent the purposeful phylogenetic movements of body handling which are the basis of survival skills. They are generally well established by age six. The modification and/or combination of these patterns into specific movement performances which require the achievement of speed, distance, and precision (or any one of these) is classified as a movement skill. The non-locomotor and locomotor skills are not restricted to phylogeny but are also representative of modification imposed by socio-cultural activity demands. The sensori-motor requisites represent abilities specific to body awareness, body in relation to surrounding objects, discrimination, and movement communication.

4.10 <u>Sensori-Motor Abilities</u>.

Those abilities which involve integration of sensory input for motor output result in a motor act or movement. The involvement of proprioceptive functioning and sense organ functioning into perceptual-motor matching are essential elements of sensori-motor abilities.

4.11 <u>Body Awareness</u>: The ability to recognize the separateness and wholeness of the body and its segments and limbs; recognition of size and form (shape) of the body; feelings regarding one's body structure (body image) and one's body movement performance; recognition of and ability in unilateral and bilateral and cross-lateral movements as well as segmental movements.

4.12 <u>Body in Relation to Space</u>: The ability to perceive the amount of space required for one's body in a variety of positions and movements; recognition of and ability to

20

select appropriate body position and/or locomotor pattern or skill to perform in a variety of space types (large, small, wide, narrow, high, low and combinations of these).

4.13 Body in Relation to Surrounding Objects: The ability to perceive size, shape, distance of objects (things, people) in near and far space and the ability to move effectively and efficiently among these objects without loss of control of own body.

4.14 Discrimination: Those abilities related to functioning of sense organs and proprioceptors required for understanding the limits within which movement can take place and which determine the movement that can be performed.

4.141 Auditory: The ability to determine differences in intensity, tone, timing, kinds of sounds and the origins of sounds in near and far space; the ability to use this information for body movement cueing.

4.142 Visual: The ability to separate figure from background and to track moving objects (ocular pursuit) in three-dimensional space both when the body is in a stationary and a moving posture; the ability to use this information for body movement cueing.

4.143 Tactile: The ability to distinguish via the skin receptors differences in texture, size and shape of objects and surfaces and to use this information for body movement cueing.

4.144 Kinesthetic: The ability to determine without auditory, visual or tactile cues the positioning of the body and its parts; the ability to use this information in movement cueing. The environment may be devoid of one or several of the auditory, visual or tactile cues, but it is never devoid of all of these cues outside of an artificial laboratory condition. As evidenced by figural after-effect following sudden cue changes, kinesthetic adaptivity allows for body positioning adjustment.

4.20 Non-locomotor Patterns and Skills.

These patterns and skills are sometimes called balance patterns or skills because they involve purposeful movements of the body and/or its parts in what appears to be a stationary position.

4.21 Total body: The ability to control one's posture in sitting, standing (including movements of body inversion) and lying positions.

4.22 <u>Body parts and segments</u>: The ability to make controlled adjustments of body parts and segments throughout specific non-locomotor tasks such as bending, straightening, stretching, twisting, rotating, and swinging.

4.30 <u>Locomotor Patterns and Skills</u>.

The locomotor patterns and skills are those purposeful movements which transport the body from one place to another. Included are movements to and through body inversion as well as walking, running, hopping, leaping, jumping, crawling, climbing, rolling, sliding, galloping and skipping. Galloping and skipping are sometimes classified as skills rather than patterns since they represent combinations and modifications of other patterns.

4.31 <u>Propulsion</u>: The ability to coordinate (synchronize) those elements necessary for initiating and executing transport of the body from one place to another; e.g., flexion and extension of joints, displacement of center of gravity beyond the base of support.

4.32 <u>Absorption</u>: The ability to coordinate (synchronize) those elements necessary for control of the forces of gravity and the momentum of the body in transport of the body from one place to another; e.g., time, surface, distance, and direction considerations.

4.40 <u>Combining Locomotor and Non-locomotor Patterns and Skills</u>.

Requisite to the performance of some specific skills found in activities such as dance and gymnastics is the ability to effectively add one or more of the non-locomotor skills to a locomotor skill.

4.41 <u>Arm Movements</u>: The ability to perform movements of the arms such as swinging, pushing, jabbing, slashing, punching, or combinations of these movements while performing a locomotor movement.

4.42 <u>Segmental Movements</u>: The ability to perform body segment movements such as bending, straightening, stretching, twisting, rotating, and swinging or combinations of these movements while performing a locomotor movement.

4.50 <u>Combining Locomotor, Non-locomotor and Body Awareness</u>.

Inherent in the performance of non-locomotor and locomotor movements are the requisites of control of body parts and body segments working separately and together, and control of body weight and momentum to a state of equilibrium.

4.51 <u>Laterality</u>: The ability to perform unilateral, bilateral, and cross-lateral movements during simultaneous non-locomotor and locomotor skill performance.

4.52   Balance: The ability to control the center-of-gravity
       of a body part, body segment, and/or the total body
       during simultaneous locomotor and non-locomotor move-
       ments with unilateral, bilateral, or cross-lateral move-
       ments of body parts.

4.60   Movement Communication.

Inherent in every movement is the attitude and amplitude of
the initiator. As the child moves, changes occur in his experience, constructs, and aptitudes. As the child's observer
or censor communicates, the child speaks to himself inter-
polatively through his own movement. Thus, the human draws
his life actively out of self and into others and this is also
true in reverse. It is a learning, teaching, and communication process that is present in all movement.

4.61   Imitative: The degree of imitative expression is rel-
       ative to the need for primal communication. The lessons
       of events and experiences of others are spoken to one-
       self by the reiteration of movements. Furthermore, the
       repetition of one's own movement defines the experience
       and makes functional one's expression.

4.62   Expressive: The degree and precision of this form of
       movement communication is reliant upon the modality
       requisites of pattern and skill acquisition. The neo-
       natal expressive forms are the roots of the movement
       art communication forms. The process may be for self
       and/or others. This is true for all communication move-
       ment processes.

4.63   Interpretative: This is, perhaps, the key mode in the
       learning-communication process. It is the explanation
       mediator for self or others, relied upon totally when
       no verbal generalizabel form is known.

5.0   OBJECT HANDLING DEVELOPMENT

The category of Object Handling Development encompasses the
propulsive patterns and skills of throwing, hitting, blocking,
pushing, pulling, and lifting. Catching is the only true absorptive
pattern or skill. The requisites of these patterns and skills are:
sensori-motor abilities, specific eye-hand and eye-foot coordina-
tions and specific elements of propulsion and absorption.

5.10   Sensori-Motor Abilities.

The involvement of proprioceptive functioning and sense organ
functioning into perceptual motor matching are essential elements of sensori-motor abilities. Refer to category 4.10 for
description of the sensori-motor abilities of Body Handling.
Additional requisites are included below.

5.11   Visual Discrimination: Ability to separate figure from
       background and to track moving objects in three dimen-
       sional space; the ability to use this information for
       body movement cueing when propelling or receiving ob-
       jects.

5.12   Auditory Discrimination: Ability to determine dif-
       ferences in intensity, timing, kinds of sounds and
       origins of sounds in near and far space; the ability to
       use this information for body movement cueing in pro-
       pelling and receiving objects.

5.13   Tactile Discrimination: The ability to distinguish via
       the skin receptors differences in texture, size, shape
       and weight of objects and to use this information for
       body movement cueing in propelling and receiving ob-
       jects.

5.14   Kinesthetic: The ability to determine without auditory,
       visual, or tactile cues the positioning of the body and
       its parts as well as the speed, force, and the extent
       of movement of the body and its parts; the ability to
       use this information in movement cueing in propelling
       and receiving objects.

5.20 Coordination.

Refers to the ability to coordinate visual or sensory interpretation of an object and the activity of the object by the
body or a body part.

5.21   Eye-hand: The ability to coordinate the visually or
       sensorially perceived object with movements of the
       hand(s) to insure control in the propulsion and receipt
       of the object.

5.22   Eye-foot: The ability to coordinate the visually or
       sensorially perceived object with movements of the foot
       (feet) to insure control in the propulsion and receipt
       of the object.

5.30 Propulsion.

Object propulsion is dependent upon the level of eye-hand and
eye-foot coordination in the achievement of accuracy, distance, and speed.

5.31   Accuracy: Placement of a propelled object (without
       variation to right, left, above or below) at desired
       location through utilization of appropriate amount of
       force, and timing for object being propelled with the
       specific pattern or skill being employed and for the
       distance required.

5.32 Distance: Placement of a propelled object at the desired distance through utilization of appropriate amount of force and timing for the object being propelled with the specific pattern or skill being employed.

5.33 Speed: The summation of forces of body movements, limb movements (and implement movement) to achieve a desired speed in the propulsion of a specific object.

5.40 Absorption.

Refers to the reduction of kinetic energy of an oncoming object for control of object and avoidance of rebounding through increase in time and distance over which object travels, and increase in surface contacting the object.

5.41 Hand: Ability to coordinate movements of the hand(s) to receive and control an oncoming object.

5.42 Implement: Ability to control movements of an implement held in the hand (as in a baseball glove) to receive and control an oncoming object.

6.0 COORDINATED BODY AND OBJECT HANDLING DEVELOPMENT

The category of Coordinated Body and Object Handling Development encompasses those performances which combine the locomotor aspect of body handling with the absorptive and propulsive aspects of object handling. Included in this category are carrying and the many specific movement skills inherent in sports and dance. Sensori-motor aspects are the same as those basic to body handling and object handling and are not reiterated.

6.10 Coordination.

Refers to eye-hand and eye-foot coordination refinements required when locomotion is combined with any object handling pattern or skill.

6.11 Eye-hand-locomotion: Modification in timing and positioning of the body and/or hands (or implement in hands) as well as adjustments in visual discrimination to compensate for the addition of body momentum.

6.12 Eye-foot-locomotion: Modification in timing and positioning of the body and/or feet as well as adjustments in visual discrimination and balance to compensate for the addition of body momentum.

6.20 Propulsion of Object-Locomotion.

6.21 Accuracy: Placement of an object at the desired location requires additional adjustments in timing of

movement of the limbs (or implement) and point of
release of the object as well as in the amount of force
applied to compensate for the addition of momentum of
the body in locomotion.

6.22   Distance: Placement of an object at the desired distance requires additional adjustments in the timing of
summation of forces of the limbs (and implement) as well
as the amount of force applied and the point of release
of the object to compensate for the addition of the
body's momentum.

6.23   Speed: The addition of locomotion requires adjustments
in the amount of force applied and the timing of the
summation of forces for release of the object.

6.30   Object Absorption-Locomotion.

6.31   Control of body weight: The initiation and/or slowing
of the body to incorporate object absorption necessi-
tates adjustments in balance for the body (and implement), in speed of body movement and movement of the
hands (and implement), and in placement of the body and
hands (and implement) to compensate for the force of the
body's momentum and the oncoming object.

6.32   Control of object force: Adjustments in amount of
distance and time as well as in the amount of surface
presented to reduce the kinetic energy of the oncoming
object are dependent upon the direction and amount of
the body's forward momentum. Moving toward the object
requires adjustments in joint flexion and/or body
segment rotation (thereby increasing distance and time)
and increase in absorptive surface to compensate for
the reduction of time and distance caused by the body's
forward momentum. Locomotion away from the oncoming
object decreases the force of the object and therefore
requires fewer adjustments for increase of time and
distance for absorption but increases the need for
visual discrimination adjustments as more time is
allowed for outside forces (gravity, air currents) to
act upon and thereby change the speed and direction of
the object.

Chapter Four

Application of the Taxonomy

The main use of the taxonomy is to provide an heuristic avenue for the user to escape from the activity planning and direct their goals to children. Activities should always be considered second to the needs of children. Rhetoric has been paid to this position, but, in truth, "what am I going to do today" was and unfortunately still is a blanket planning statement. It is hoped that the taxonomy provides an holistic view of what children need to grow. The reader in scanning the taxonomy, should be constantly considering each child in reference to his needs and with this consideration, build a program for the individual child and groups of children reflecting those selected items. This book is not a cook book of games and activities, and the reader is advised to use such "how to" tomes for the selection of appropriate activities only after the objectives meeting the needs of children have been carefully formulated.

The taxonomy is offered as an alternative for teachers who plan activities rather than planning for children. It also provides an alternative system of selecting objectives for the teachers who utilize the terminal and tightly closed objective considerations of how many, or how far, or how fast. The child is unique. His performance is comparable to others, but more importantly, his performance today is comparable to his past performance. If the individual child is the educator's business, then recording and comparing individual progress is mandated. The taxonomy offers a guide for this process.

Further use of the taxonomy is concerned with developing a physical education program that weathers the storm of accountability. Accountability has become an economic reality to all educators and is here to stay for the present and future of education. In physical education, small concerns should be spent on how many games any child knows, and large concerns should be directed toward the growth and development a child has achieved from having experienced the game, the psychomotor environment, or the motor situation. Justification for program can be directly related to the taxonomy. An example of this is to establish a measure of a child's understanding of his limitations, (item 2.21) have him select a partner of equal ability for catching and throwing a ball. His partner's skill similarity indicates the child's concept of self in relation to reality.

The taxonomy is not hierarchically arranged, but classifies broad concepts for which objectives can be written by the elementary staff that provide integration of all subject areas to the benefit of the child. In the preschool situations with which the authors have been involved, all staff of various specialities arrive at common objectives prior to formulating actual learning experiences for the children. For some unknown reason, this has not been observed in elementary schools. The doors of planning communications have not been opened to the concerns of the whole child. The physical domain belongs to physical education and the cognitive domain belongs to the classroom teacher. The social-emotional domain seems to be shared by all with direction spurious at best. The classification system should provide impetus for the physical educator to become more aware of the cognitive aspects of psychomotor experiences of children and the development of curricula reflecting the cognitive functioning of children. The social-emotional development is not a sea unto itself as the social development of children is certainly dependent upon and tightly matrixed with the motor and mental development of the child. Again, objectives constructed for the benefit of children should be widened considerably by using the classification system and the selection of learning experiences should reflect the social-emotional development. Communications between the classroom teacher, other elementary specialists, and the physical educator must be not only available, but also in fine tune to reach the needs of children and facilitate their development.

The designers of the taxonomy have, to a large extent, limited its application to knowledges, values and performances related to human movement (psychomotor development). This should not be interpreted as promotion of physical education program separation from the total educational program, but simply reflects the expertise of the designers. The material included incorporates concepts from other subject areas, suggestions for both initial concept learning and concept reinforcement, as well as affective and psychomotor goals which are applicable for the total curriculum. For full realization of the potential of education, all subject area teachers, including physical educators must work together in determining appropriate goals for children and implementing the total curriculum (preschool and elementary school).

No reference to sex is included in the taxonomy. If the objectives of physical education are valuable for one sex child, they are valuable for the opposite sexed child as well. No legal ruling could change the belief in the values held for all children. Sex role identification is an important function in development, having been more important in the past and seemingly less important today and probably even less important in the future. The Hazelwood program presented in this book reflects views different from the authors and does utilize the taxonomy for building and defending differing values for boys and girls. The taxonomy as a document holds within it the flexibility or the rigidity of the user, but sex differences were not considered as a base in construction.

One of the features of the taxonomy that can be advantageous is the possibility for cross-referencing. Cross-referencing is seen when items from various categories are grouped in clusters of objectives. An example of this would be to have constructed behavioral objectives from the following taxonomic items:

Taxonomic item: Behavioral objective.

1.11   Body parts and body segments: Learner will demonstrate rec-
       ognition and understanding of changes in center of gravity,
       summation of forces in running with quick directional changes.

1.66   Social science: Learner will demonstrate understanding of and
       concern for rules of a game.

2.11   Enjoyment in physical endeavor: Learner will evidence en-
       joyment in participating in an activity requiring running and
       evading or tagging another person.

2.13   Participation in movement activities: Learner will evidence
       willingness to participate in an activity requiring running
       and evading or tagging another person.

2.22   Body image: Learner will demonstrate awareness of his size
       and ability in running, tagging and evading in relation to
       his classmates.

2.23   Self-discipline: Learner will evidence willingness to admit
       being tagged without teacher or peer pressure.

3.11   Stop and start: Learner will demonstrate the ability to
       terminate movement quickly while running without loss of
       balance or control.

4.13   Body in relation to surrounding objects: Learner will demon-
       strate the ability to run efficiently among other people
       making directional changes without loss of control of his own
       body.

4.32   Absorption: Learner will demonstrate the ability to control
       gravitational forces and his own body momentum in running,
       tagging, and evading others.

One movement experience "line tag" was selected to meet the above
objectives. (Line tag is a chasing and fleeing game where all
participants must stay on lines of the gymnasium while fleeing from
one person who is initially "it". The "it" illustrates his
authority by holding his hand high in the air at all times ((or by
some other body part discrimination technique)). "It" tags any
player who then shares the authority to tag other players. The
cumulative tag game terminates when all players are "it".) Changing
line tag to almost any tag game would reinforce the same related
taxonomic items and behavioral objectives.

       In the course of a normal lesson, two or three primary ob-
jectives are usually selected. The illustration of items and objectives met by line tag are elaborated to emphasize the utility
process inherent in the taxonomic structure.

       Gross referencing should indicate an holistic program for
children. It is difficult to select an item of the taxonomy, build
a learner objective and avoid alluding to any taxonomic item from

another category. Use and growing awareness of the taxonomy should lead curriculum planners to matrixing items fit for the learner. Concerted efforts are necessary to direct a physical education program toward the development of a totally developed child.

One might also design a behavioral objective for one taxonomic item and select several learning experiences directed toward the attainment of that objective. It is possible to select a cluster of several taxonomic items, design objectives for them, and then design or select several learning experiences directed toward the attainment of the objectives. This technique is most often utilized when the time allotment for learner attainment of the objectives is for several days or for a two, or three week period of time.

The taxonomy is presented as an idea stimulant for program planning. While reading the taxonomy, items may be seen that have not been the concern of the curriculum planner. The promotion of those items in curriculum should serve to enrich that curriculum for children.

Further, related items in crossed-referenced curriculum facilitates comprehensive evaluation. Justification of any program is relative to the number and kinds of benefits derived by children from experiences presented within that program. The inclusion of cross-referenced objectives should lead to cross-referenced evaluation items and therefore evaluation reflecting the broad spectrum of curricular offerings.

Chapter Five

Curriculum Development

Curriculum development at the elementary school level should be a cooperative enterprise. In too many instances the physical educator is called upon to provide a program of instruction with no input from or concern of the teachers of the other subject areas in the elementary school. Ideally, the response of the physical educator to a request to design a physical education curriculum for a school would be to in turn ask for a committee to assist. A committee composed of the physical educator(s), elementary classroom teachers, and where germaine, other subject area specialists, should ensure both continuity and concurrence in the selection and teaching of concepts across the entire elementary school curriculum. In the event that a formal committee structure is not realized, the individual(s) designing the physical education curriculum should enlist the assistance of the elementary classroom teachers in a review of the curriculum design and solicit assistance in making the physical education curriculum congruent with the total elementary curriculum. In either situation, the following step-wise progression in curriculum development is suggested.

Steps in Curriculum Development

1. Determination of the educational philosophy of the school and its congruence with current elementary education and physical education philosophy. (Through discussion with administration, current curriculum guide for the school, school handbook, etc.).

2. Needs Assessment: Determination of needs of the target pupil population based on application of data obtained by empirical observation, literature, and research review.

3. Development of behavioral expectations for target population in light of needs assessment and concept expectations for the total elementary curriculum.

4. Selection of an objectives' classification system (taxonomy).

5. Design of objectives for the taxonomic categories to span all levels included in the target elementary school.

6. Selection of taxonomic items per grade level in light of needs assessment to ensure appropriate balance among taxonomic categories.

7. Selection and modification of behavioral objectives within the taxonomic categories (see #5 above) for specific grade levels.

8. Design and selection of learning experiences to meet behavioral objectives for all grade levels.

9. Arrangement of objectives and corresponding learning experiences into a yearly program across grades and in relation to the entire elementary education curriculum.

   Note: Daily lesson plans fit into this step but it is rarely feasible to design these more than a week ahead if pupil progress toward the attainment of objectives is being considered.

10. Curriculum evaluation should be ongoing throughout the year with in depth evaluation at the end of the school year. In each instance evaluation should be in light of the extent of the learners' attainment of the objectives.

11. Curriculum revisions both of a minor and major nature should be based on the data obtained through evaluation process.

Step-wise progression in curriculum planning provides the designer with direction, but there are many more considerations the authors wish to convey. Placement of those considerations is assigned to this chapter, which may confuse the reader until such time as the Hazelwood School District development examples are reviewed. It is not the intent to confuse, rather to elaborate for clarity. It is suggested that after reading the remaining pages in this chapter, the reader go on to chapters 6 through 9 and then return to reread this entire chapter.

Physical education is education of the physical and through the physical. Children constantly involve themselves in active examination of their worlds. The extent to which experience variety is provided governs the balance or imbalance of the cognitive, affective, and psychomotor development levels in children. Bruner (1964) illustrates the development of communications when he refers to enactive, iconic and symbolic representation. The enactive mode is physical expression, the iconic mode is pictorial, and the symbolic mode is verbal expression. The physical, pictorial, and verbal modes are also concerned with the process of learning and teaching. When one knows nothing of a thing, the only way to know it is to become physically involved with it. When one has had physical involvement with a thing, that physical experience can serve as knowledge from which pictorial generalizations can be made. Pictorial representations can be coded into a verbal system by which all past experience can be recounted. The epitome of representation is verbal coding, but the origin of understanding is physical. The author is reminded of the Ferguson-Florissant School District (St. Louis County, Mo.) and the elementary school remedial summer program wherein her students provided physical activity experiences in math, reading, and language arts for children suffering difficulty in learning in those areas under traditional methods. The Thompson-Mann taxonomy was the stem for this program dealing with over 200 children per year, and it was successful as witnessed through repeated requests from the aforementioned district to

continue the program. Children who do not have sufficient physical/
sensorial experience with a specific knowledge cannot accommodate
that knowledge until that physical/sensorial experience is provided.

Physical (enactive) experience should be provided by any
teacher attempting to educate children, and the physical educator
should be thoroughly acquainted with the physical modalities incorporated in learning. The physical educator should provide experiences to meet objectives in any academic area in which the
child needs physical experiences, but, those academic experiences
provided directly by the physical educator should be those that involve large muscle and vigorous movement. In this way both academic
and motor development objectives are being considered.

In developing behavioral objectives from the taxonomy, the
reader should be well aware of the child's developmental levels in
the three domains, psychomotor, cognitive, and affective. Keeping
those levels in mind, selection of activities (learning experiences)
should be congruent. The whole child is a matrix of these three
domains and that matrix is unique to that child and different for
all other children. Kephart (1960) mentioned the term splintering
as a referrent for one who has developed handicapping physical
specificity of function. Splintering is viewed by the authors in
the limited sense of physical performance specificity and as a
broader term encompassing the idea of domain splintering. In the
narrow sense, one who is splintered may be a fine baseball pitcher
and at the same time a poor football passer. We have seen skilled
athletes incapable of writing or speaking intelligently of their
performances and we have seen college professor, skilled in communications, yet unskilled in simple motor endeavors. Both the
athlete and professor were splintered. The athlete was splintered
toward development of the psychomotor domain over the cognitive
domain, and the professor was splintered toward the cognitive
domain over the psychomotor domain. Splintering may occur as a
result of environmental or genetic propensities. Splintering occurs
also as a result of acceptance and reward. Being favored in one
area, the child's interests may become intense only to that area
and to the expense and exclusion of all other interests. The motor
and cognitive growth differences between girls and boys can be
hypothetically charged to splintering as a result of societal expectation and encouragement.

It is within the teacher's responsibility to promote a balance
of domains and to promote the processes of generalizations. Specificity of function is a biological truth that can be utilized toward the promotion of generalization. A specific function learned
can be utilized in a function of similar components. The elementary
school teacher must be able to realize component similarities and
involve the child in experiences that will promote generalizations.

Determination of the developmental level for each of the
domains for each child is an essential procedure if one is to promote equity among the three domains. Despite the inadequacy of
instrumentation in this regard, it is still possible to gather
sufficient developmental information to enable the parent or teacher
to promote balance among the three domains. The collection and

compilation of information into a cumulative record for each child is a very satisfactory procedure if the information is then utilized in planning learning experiences for the child. The taxonomy should serve as a referrent for avoidance of splintering, both in the narrow and broad sense of the word. The taxonomy is meant to encompass the broad benefits facilitated in physical education.

One must guard against the assignment of percentages of time to specific activities or units in the area of motor development. So also must the designers of elementary school curriculum avoid the assignment of specific amounts of time devoted to specific subject areas. Rather one must again take into consideration the developmental needs of the age group and the individual children within the age group and determine the concepts most appropriate for them. The next step involves identification of the variety of so-called subject areas which can be utilized to elicit understanding of and increase in the ability of the child to apply the concept. Such procedures should result in the cooperation of all areas, including physical education in selecting meaningful ways to promote the concept through each subject area in a manner that will reach all children. It seems therefore ridiculous in curriculum planning and lesson planning in any subject area, to attempt to establish set amounts of time (minutes per week or time percentages) to be allotted that subject. As could be extracted from the foregoing, it may be more important for instance, for greater amounts of time in the child's school day to be spent on certain math, science, and motor development concepts than on spelling, music, reading, or language arts per se, but all can be involved in the teaching of the concepts needing emphasis at a particular time.

It is time the view of integration of subject areas through artificially concocted experiences is eliminated from curriculum planning. All experiences should be meaningful to the child and designed to assist in the assimilation of knowledges and skills presented to him. Concepts which are best presented and most easily assimilated by the child through movement experiences should be so presented without concern that the concept falls in the realm of science, math, social science or language arts, etc. Elaboration for better understanding of specific concepts should be delegated to those areas best able to achieve it. The concern is for development of the child, not equality of time among subject areas. Physical education then, as other subject areas, becomes a vehicle for enhancing the child's learning rather than a specific set of knowledges and proficiencies separate from the rest of the curriculum. Cooperative planning among all subject areas must be made in light of the concepts to be taught, the differences in the ways children learn, individual and group developmental differences (all aspects of development), individual differences in values and value systems acceptance, and in light of the effectiveness of various learning settings.

The selection of items from the taxonomic categories and the arrangement of them in a curricular structure should reflect progression throughout the grade levels. Such progression must be based, at each level, on the needs of the population for which the curriculum is being designed. The set of Behavioral Expectations included in Chapter seven illustrates one method of arranging the taxonomic items to reflect progression for use in writing objectives and selecting learning experiences.

The curriculum building novice frequently pages through the elementary school physical education activity "cook books" to select the physical education menu for the day. This is an unjustified planning procedure which must be eliminated. It is, of course, possible to use the taxonomy in the same irresponsible manner. The curriculum thus designed may in initial appearance seem to be sound when in fact it is not. Evaluation of curriculum content is essential to avoid the empty shell offerings of the unprofessional manipulators of children and tax dollars.

Inherent in the numbering system of the taxonomy is the potential for item analyses and consequently validation. Such study is in progress and the authors look forward to further collaboration on it. The Hazelwood Charts reflect the loading of factors considered for various age/developmental groupings. Statistical charts should be even more valuable in summarizing past directions and future trend.

Accountability is of interest to all readers. As the reader selects the items for construction of objectives, he should remember that the acquisition of competencies reflecting the objectives for the learner should be measurable in the taxonomic stem from which the objective came. In the development of an objective for item 1.11 (recognition and identification of body parts and segments), the following is posed:

Objective: Learner will demonstrate knowledge of the location and names of body parts.

Learning Experience: "Busy Bee"   (This is a game with players in pairs, Leader calls body part: knee, toe, head, etc. Pairs join those parts. Leader calls "Busy Bee" which indicates that each player seek a new partner and resume jointure of body parts. Three or more body parts are called between "Busy Bee" calls.)

Evaluation: Learner responds correctly/incorrectly to calls.

The evaluative item is in "check list" format. A "yes" or "no" for this evaluation item and selected other items should serve to identify what a child can or cannot do. As the Hazelwood Charts suggest, certain categories are considered more important for certain age/development children. Evaluative items therefore should reflect concentrations of objectives when using a check list. The assignment of value range is also possible. Changing the evaluative item from the above illustration and adding a sliding scale allows even deeper insights of the child's performance.

Construction of objectives designed for particular children or groups of children should be done simultaneously with the construction of evaluative items. Individual charts could be maintained for each child but this process could be a time consumer. Spot checking is more in keeping with the taxonomy. Randomization techniques in evaluation processes should prove fruitful for the purpose of establishing accountability. Controlled random selection of subjects tested on items capable of reflecting wide variance in performance is a desirable evaluative method.

In the selection of experiences to meet appropriate behavioral objectives for elementary school children, the following activity guidelines are presented. These guides not only aid in forming appropriate learning experiences but also should be used in evaluation of any particular learning experience presented to children. The curriculum is as strong as each of its selected learning experiences for each child. Both the total and parts of the curriculum must be considered for strengthening the elementary physical education offerings.

Activity Guidelines

1. Do the activities promote physical vigor? Include large muscle movement.

2. Do the activities contribute to fine motor control?

3. Do the activities promote positive self-concept for all children? (No elimination games, no individual defeat/frustration).

4. Do the activities promote equal and ample participation?

5. Do the children enjoy the activity?

6. Does the activity stop at a high participation point. Don't wear it to tedium.

7. Is the relationship of the activity to the behavioral objective clear to the learners?

8. Do the activities allow the children opportunities to communicate in verbal, symbolic and physical modes?

9. Do the activities allow for the arbitration process?

10. Are explanations brief and clear?

11. Does the sequence of activities presented contribute to the children's effectiveness in dealing with the total school program? (Maturing, calming, ready to learn).

12. Do the activities fit the affective, cognitive, and psycho-motor development levels of the children?

Chapter Six

Development of the Hazelwood Curriculum

The Hazelwood Curriculum was developed by the task force of ten physical educators in consultation with the authors of the taxonomy. Utilizing a set of behavioral expectations provided by the authors, behavioral objectives were formulated for each sub-category of the taxonomy, and learning experiences were selected for each objective to assist the learner in accomplishing the objectives. Objectives were stated in an open-ended manner. This enabled the curriculum designers to utilize them across developmental levels, as well as over an extended period of time. Listing of learning experiences for each of the objectives was then accomplished in a developmental hierarchial fashion, making them usable across levels within a specific objective.

In light of developmental information and partially guided by the results of the Gordon, Alspaugh, and Thompson study (1973), objectives were selected for specific grade levels. These objectives were arranged on a continuum, where appropriate, for the school year. Care was taken to select congruent objectives from the various categories for a given time period. For example, a mental development objective was matched with a physical development and/or body handling development objective. Likewise, the mental development objective might be matched with a social-emotional development objective and/or an object handling development objective. The foregoing is an example of cross-referencing, but it is not necessary or reasonable to match each objective with an objective from each of the other objective categories.

The Curriculum Chart represents groups of related objectives among the categories and groups of objectives within a category that indicate progression in that category for the learner. As one moves from week one through week thirty-two and as one compares grade Kindergarten through grade six, progressions should be noted in the objectives. Further, the experiences selected to meet the objectives should also be arranged in a manner which indicates progression for the learner.

It should be noted that the curriculum chart was designed for use by thirty-eight teachers in nineteen schools in the Hazelwood School District. Therefore, provision of groups of objectives and varying the length of time to meet them allows flexibility per school. Differences in facilities, equipment, and student population thus can be facilitated. In using the chart each school might select different experiences to meet objectives but adherence to the total curriculum should prevail. In many instances a single learning experience may be used to attain several objectives. This is shown in the cross-referencing in the Hazelwood Charts of

Objectives and Learning Experiences for each taxonomic category. The following examples of these phenomena may help clarify the points for the reader.

The Use of A Variety of Experiences to Meet the Same Objective

2.124 The learner shall demonstrate an awareness of movement activity participation as an avenue for self-expression and self-realization.

A. Using Ball Handling Skills (this example was designed for grades 3-5). Each child with a ball will experiment with the following tasks or ideas:

bouncing the ball moving in different directions
bouncing the ball with right hand, left hand, alternating hands
bouncing the ball at different levels
bouncing the ball and turning around before retrieving it
bouncing the ball under one leg
creating a routine utilizing the above skills
creating new skills (behind the back, across front from rt. to left)

B. Using Lummi Sticks (this example was designed for grades 1-3)*

down / down / hit / hit
tap right / tap left / tap right / tap left
tap right / hit / tap left / hit
down / down / flip right
down / down / flip left
play add on (each person adds a new task)
make own routine by putting several of these together by oneself or with a partner or with three persons
perform the above tasks while incorporating movements of body: from sitting to kneeling, twisting the trunk, incorporating locomotor patterns

*Each child with two lummi sticks experiments with the above tasks to a four beat count. The terms used are defined as follows:

down = hitting both sticks on the floor simultaneously
hit = hitting both sticks together
tap = tap one stick on floor
flip = toss one stick in air and catch it

C. Using Pyramid Building (designed for grade five)-Groups of 5-8

Design and build a pyramid with the base larger than the top

Design and build a pyramid with the top larger than
the base
Design and build a pyramid with a stationary base and one
part moving
Design and build a moving pyramid
Incorporate one of the pyramid designs with that of
another group

The Use of One Experience to Meet Several Objectives

1.122 Understanding of self in general space and in varying space
sizes without obstacles.

1.221 Understanding of self in general space and in varying space
sizes with obstacles.

2.112 Enjoyment of participation in established and novel psychomotor events.

3.13 Ability to make rapid changes from one level to another in a
controlled manner while performing a locomotor or non-
locomotor pattern; change locomotor pattern while changing
levels.

4.121 Ability to change body shape in relation to size and shape of
space that one's body is to occupy.

4.132 Ability to perform locomotor patterns and skills among people
or objects without bumping and without losing balance in
changing spaces.

Using An Obstacle Course - maze of ropes, hoops, pole to go under,
pole to go over, tunnel made of mats,
large object to get over, balance board
or beam to walk. Use of directional
cards and complexity of design dependent
upon developmental level.

Children go through course with task cards or can do problem
solving:

First task - start at any point in obstacle course and go
through
Second task - change locomotor pattern and/or direction
Third task - respond to drum beat's cue change for speed as
traverse obstacle course
Fourth task - traverse the obstacle course with a partner
Fifth task - children make up own obstacle course to meet
above objectives.

The foregoing examples can be transposed to the use of any
body handling and object handling activities with and without response to imposed rhythm and for any developmental level. The experiences can be designed for any organizational pattern (partners,

groups, mass, individual working alone) but should always provide for individualization within the organizational pattern.

The charts of the Hazelwood Behavioral Objectives and Learning Experiences should serve the reader as a further guide for developing a full curriculum. The Curriculum Charts and Behavioral Objectives and Learning Experiences designed by the physical education task force may warrant considerable alterations for the purpose of serving the reader. It is hoped the examples from the Hazelwood School District Curriculum will be used as models and not adopted intact. There is no intent to sell a packaged curriculum as the authors fully embrace the concept that a curriculum designed for one school or district will not exactly fit the needs of another school or district. Hazelwood presents a five days per week program of physical education for each child. Basic schedules differ from district to district and even school to school. Facilities and equipment are not identical in all schools, and there may be some differences in educational philosophy among teachers which may influence curriculum content from school to school.

Chapter Seven

Behavioral Expectations by Category

The behavioral expectations by category section was designed by the authors. This chapter represents two lifetimes of practice with and study of children. It was presented to the Hazelwood curriculum planners as a device to increase the understanding of how the taxonomy could be used as a base for curriculum development.

The behavioral expectations provided the clarity necessary for the planners to work with the authors toward the production of the taxonomic based Hazelwood curriculum. It is hoped that this chapter provides the same direction for the readers.

1.0 MENTAL DEVELOPMENT CATEGORY BEHAVIORAL EXPECTATIONS

1.10 Knowledge and Understanding of the Human Body

    1.11 Review identification by name of body parts in light of right and left sides of body, and part location (upper/lower)

    1.12 Identify body segments (refer to body part locations)

        1.121 Body part and segments in relation to concepts of: over-under, above-below, between, behind-in front of, near-far, forward-backward, up-down, sideward, long-short.

        1.122 Body part, body segments and total body in relation to concepts of: near-far space, open-restricted space, wide-narrow space, high-low space, tall-short space.

        1.123 Body parts, body segments in relation to concepts of range of movement: large, small.

        1.124 Body parts, body segments in relation to concepts of quality of movement: fast-slow, strong-light, sustained-percussive, direct-indirect (time, flow, force, direction).

1.20 Knowledges and Understandings of Movement Patterns and Skills

    1.21 Pattern and Skill Terminology

        1.211 Name and differentiate among patterns and skills:

            1.2111 Locomotor skills: walk, run, hop, leap, jump, gallop, skip, fall, land.

            1.2112 Non-locomotor skills: bend, stretch, curl, twist, rotate, swing, push, pull.

            1.2113 Balances: upright, inverted, points, patches.

1.2114 Object Propulsion/Receipt Skills:

(one hand/both hands) Throwing: overhand, underhand, push/swing patterns, roll, toss, pass, shoot for basket.

Catching: overhead, below waist, to side, chest level

Hitting: bounce, dribble, volley, pass, serve, block

Hitting/Implement: serve, bat, pass, dribble, smash, lob, shoot

(using the feet) Kicking: trapping, rebounding, passing, punting, place kicking, drop-kicking

(using the body) Blocking: head, shoulder, chest, body surfaces

Rebounding: head, shoulder, chest, body surfaces

1.212 Differentiate among movement terms: leverage, stance, flexion, extension, backswing, follow-through, time, force, flow (free-bound), stop, start, change direction, space (near, far, own, self, general).

1.213 Differentiate among formations: single file, single line side by side, parallel lines, lines facing, circle, double circle, clockwise, counter-clockwise, square, triangle, pairs, threes, etc.

1.214 Differentiate among strategy terms: guarding variations for basketball, football, soccer, hockey; ready position for tennis, receiving a pass, starting a sprint, jumping for a tossed ball, etc.

1.215 Differentiate among dance steps: two-step, polka, schottische, waltz, dance turns, bleking, etc.

1.216 Differentiate among tumbling/gymnastic terms: headstand, handstand, tip-up, tripod, mule-kick, cartwheel, crabwalk, rocker, handspring, kip, somersaults, walkovers, flips, vaults, pyramids, approach, spotting, etc.

1.0   MENTAL DEVELOPMENT CATEGORY BEHAVIORAL EXPECTATIONS (Continued)

1.217   Know basic water safety skills and equipment: bobbing, types of buoys, treading water, basic rules for swimming safety and boating safety, life-preserver, life-jacket, etc.

1.22   <u>Purpose and Use of Skills</u> (In relation to basic movement skills and to specific activity skills)

1.221   Movement adjustments in space with and without others and/or objects: starting, stopping, changing directions, landing, side-stepping.

1.222   Choice of locomotor pattern for different speeds, changes of level, response to specific rhythms.

1.223   Use of arm and leg opposition/same side in throwing, hitting, receipt of force

1.224   Changes of body facing for different types of throwing, hitting, receipt of force

1.225   Use of different stances for different types of throwing, hitting, receipt of force.

1.226   Use of bending-stretching (flexion/extension) in propelling self and propelling objects.

1.227   Use of extension/flexion in landing (receiving own weight) and in receiving objects.

1.228   Choice of one hand or both hands in throwing, hitting, catching.

1.229   Choice of type (overhand, underhand) throw or hit for distance, accuracy, speed, force.

1.23   <u>Pattern and Skill Continuity</u>

1.231   Adjustment of locomotor patterns for specific tasks: running on a zig-zag path, dodging an opponent or object, evading an opponent, running in a circle (various sizes), sprint running, running bases, distance running,

44

track events in jumping, jumping on a trampoline, jumping a turning rope, performing dance steps, performing dances.

1.232 Adjustment of throwing, hitting, kicking, catching for specific tasks: dribbling a ball with hands, feet, implement; kicking ball through and over goal, to a teammate; hitting ball to a specific spot for accuracy with paddle, bat, racquet, hand; catching a football, basketball, batted ball, deck-tennis ring, frisbee; throwing darts, deck-tennis ring, putting the shot, throwing a discus, throwing a javelin.

1.233 Combining body handling and object handling: dribbling while running; turning and jumping a rope oneself; rolling a hoop; hoop activities with body parts; rhythmic ball handling; spiking and blocking in volleyball; running and receiving a passed object (football, frisbee, etc.)

1.30 Knowledges and Understandings of Mechanical Principles of Movement

1.31 Locomotion

1.311 Force Production: body lean, flexion/extension of joints to produce movement, synchrony of timing, summation of forces.

1.312 Stability: Lowering center of gravity, widening base of support in relation to type surface, use of arms for balance, changing directions, changing levels with control

1.313 Force Absorption: Increasing time and distance (therefore decrease chance of injury) by presenting larger body surface, flexion at joints, continued motion in same direction as body in moving for receipt of own body weight in landings from jumps, in falls, control of forward momentum in running, skipping, etc. for stopping with control.

1.32 Body Parts

1.321 Use of increase, decrease of lever for speed, distance (see 1.31, 1.33, 1.34)

1.322 Use of flexion-extension for force production

1.323 Use of flexion for stability

1.0 MENTAL DEVELOPMENT CATEGORY BEHAVIORAL EXPECTATIONS (Continued)

1.324 Role of the arc of swing of the arm or leg in force production, direction

1.325 Use of flexion or extension of arms in balance

1.33 Propulsion of objects (all factors to be considered in relation to size, weight, mass and shape of objects)

1.331 Factors influencing distance: speed of throw or swing of implement; angle of release or impact; outside forces of gravity, air currents; synchrony of timing.

1.332 Factors influencing speed: synchrony of timing, speed of lever at time of release or impact; addition of body rotation for increased lever length; weight transfer and movement of the body in direction of action.

1.333 Factors influencing direction: angle of release; when two forces meet: direction is the resultant of the two forces; when two moving forces meet: direction is determined by the angle and the momentum of each, the direction the lever (arm, leg, implement) is moving, firmness of the striking surface; placement of striking surface in relation to the center of gravity of the object; placement on striking surface of the object.

1.34 Receipt of Objects

1.341 Factors related to Catching: Increase of time and distance by forward reach, then consecutive joint flexion of fingers, wrists and arms; addition of backward step; addition of body rotation; addition of forward trunk flexion.

1.342 Factors related to Blocking with the Body: Use of large body surface; moving in same direction as approaching object (therefore away from rather than toward object)

1.343 Factors related to Trapping (stopping): With one foot or with one knee (weight of body kept on supporting leg); force applied to ball sufficient only for control; with both knees: keep weight above base of support, apply force sufficient for ball control.

1.40 Knowledges and Understandings of Physiologic Factors

1.41 Effects of health state, emotions, relaxation, stress (tension), diet, on activity performance

1.42 Differences in performance expectations in relation to age, weight, height, etc.

1.43 Effects of exercise on heart rate, breathing, muscle tone, general feeling of well being

1.44 Increase number and/or intensity to build strength and endurance

1.45 Increase range of movement at joints by increased stretching to gain greater flexibility

1.46 Fitness level increases with activity; decreases with inactivity

1.50 Knowledges and Understandings of Rules and Strategies

1.51 Rules and Regulations for Performance for Specific Activities

1.511 Self in relation to space of others

1.512 Knowledge of what objects are to be hit, kicked, thrown

1.513 Knowledge of what kinds of activities are to be performed in specified areas; on specified equipment

1.514 Rules of specific games or other movement activities

1.52 Strategies for Specific Activities

1.521 Specific activities by oneself: throwing, rebounding objects, achieving height, distance, accuracy.

1.522 Specific activities with partner:couple stunts, ball passing, combatives, rope jumping, tether ball, rhythmic activities (lummi sticks, partner dances) in terms of body placement, use of strength, timing balance.

1.0 MENTAL DEVELOPMENT CATEGORY BEHAVIORAL EXPECTATIONS (Continued)

1.523 Specific activities in a small group: passing objects, evading opponents, achieving ready position, building pyramids, performing rhythmic activities (folk dances, marching, tinikling, ball/hoop/rope routines)

1.524 For specific movement activities with large groups (games, gymnastics, dances, relays, etc.)

1.53 Safety Factors Related to Rules and Strategies

1.531 Recognition of hazard of hitting or throwing object into group performing another activity

1.532 Recognition of hazard of running through area of group performing another activity

1.533 Recognition of hazard of improper use of equipment (hand apparatus and large apparatus)

1.534 Recognition of hazard of laughing while performing inverted and/or partner/group stunts, "horsing around" while performing activities or while others are performing activities.

1.535 Ability to determine rules to avoid injury and/or equipment damage in above situations.

1.60 Knowledges and Understandings of Common/Related Concepts

1.61 Art

1.611 Realization of body parts and total body form as similar to all forms and structures

1.612 Awareness of movement as a depth dimension of form and structure

1.613 Awareness of color and intensity as compatible factors in flow and movement

1.614 Aesthetic concepts in movement

1.615   Identification with the world of art through increasing appreciation of movement and concepts gained thereby

1.62   Language Arts

1.621   Communication of movement experiences (oral and written) for self and others

1.622   Interpretation of communication into movement forms and experiences (to know what to do from what is said or read)

1.623   Realization of the great need for syntactic and semantic abilities in learning, performing and planning movement experiences

1.624   Documentation (written evidence) of one's own movement performance and experiences

1.63   Math

1.631   Sets: the similarities and dissimilarities of those characteristics of movement and the beings that are able to move

1.632   Priorities in difficulties and degrees of movement and the changing orders through movement experiences

1.633   Measurement and records of personal movement experiences using math codes

1.634   Use of Math to aid in learning, performing, and planning movement experiences

1.635   Movement as a basis for the understanding of distance, space, time, force, and that the symbol system representing movement is the substance of mathematics

1.64   Music

1.641   Rhythm as evidence of movement experience. Sound is made in movement and can be monitored and replicated in movement(s) with timing similarities

49

1.0 MENTAL DEVELOPMENT CATEGORY BEHAVIORAL EXPECTATIONS (Continued)

1.642 Melody as the content of movement events gives meaning to a movement composition. Awareness that music is compatible to movement performance.

1.643 Utilization of music and the components of music for the purpose of learning, performing, and planning movement experiences.

1.644 Appreciation of music as sound illustrated documents of movement and time.

1.65 Science

1.651 Utilization of mathematic communication codes to describe the scientific aspects of movement experiences.

1.652 The natural boundaries described by science that delineate the possibilities of human movement experiences.

1.653 Realization of human movement experience as a predictor of science phenomena; to relate movement experience to possible events in nature.

1.654 Employment of physical laws in learning, performing, and planning human movement experiences.

1.655 The physical properties and laws of nature are inseparable from the properties and laws concerning and governing the human body and the movement of the human body.

1.66 Social Science

1.661 Realization of self values by seeing the values of others displayed in human movement experiences.

1.662 Control of self and others for the purpose of individual and coactors' achievements.

1.663 Realization of self as leader or follower and appropriateness of role as experience, group membership dictates.

1.664 Realization of group structures as a learning, performing, and planning consideration in human movement experience.

1.665 The social opportunities presented in a physical education experience provide an open-ended forum for the understanding of one's self and others. Governance and achievement are relative to coaction movement experience.

2.0 SOCIAL-EMOTIONAL DEVELOPMENT BEHAVIORAL EXPECTATIONS

2.10 Appreciation and Acceptance of Physical Activity

2.11 Enjoyment in Physical Endeavor

2.111 Appreciation as a spectator of peer performance and skilled performers in various psychomotor events (dance, swimming, tennis, golf, gymnastics, bicycling, baseball, soccer, etc.)

2.112 Enjoyment of participation in established and novel psychomotor events.

2.12 Effects of Physical Activity

2.121 A measurable concept of beneficial physiological effects of movement activity participation.

2.122 A measurable concept of movement activity participation as an avenue to socialization (partner, group, team).

2.123 A measurable concept of the role of movement activity participation as a vent for and/or alleviator of emotional tensions (sublimation potential).

2.124 A measurable concept of movement activity participation as an avenue for self-expression and self-realization.

2.13 Participation in Movement Activities

2.131 Willingness to participate in movement activities to derive pleasure.

2.132 Willingness to participate in movement activities to derive physiologic benefits (cardiorespiratory/skeletomuscular fitness).

51

2.0 SOCIAL-EMOTIONAL DEVELOPMENT BEHAVIORAL EXPECTATIONS (Continued)

    2.133 Willingness to participate in movement activities to realize socialization potential (partner, group, team).

    2.134 Willingness to participate in movement activities to realize creative expression potential (see 2.15).

2.14 Achievement of Skill and Success in Movement Activities

    2.141 Establishment of achievable goals for all movement activity participation.

    2.142 Maintenance of a positive level of aspiration within realistic scope of the performer.

2.15 Non-Verbal Communication Through Movement

    2.151 Recognition of movement as a form of communication of feelings, mood, emotions, attitudes.

    2.152 Recognition of movement as a form of communication of ideas from simple gestures and postures to sophisticated choreography in floor exercise, dances, and swimming.

    2.153 Recognition of movement of others as a means of communication to self.

2.20 Values of a Positive Self-Concept

    2.21 Abilities and Limitations

        2.211 Recognition of own movement capabilities and limitations in all movement patterns and skills.

        2.212 Willingness to examine own movement capabilities and limitations and accept them in light of own developmental level.

        2.213 Willingness to make adjustments in self-expectation based on movement behavior of peers in light of own size, weight, etc.

2.22 Body Image

    2.221 Awareness of self through the awareness of others (structure and growth).

    2.222 Awareness of potential in growth structure and performance.

    2.223 Concept of own structure in relation to movement capabilities.

    2.224 Concept of how others view one's structure and performance.

2.23 Self-Discipline

    2.231 Recognition and acceptance toward realizing responsibility for one's own behavior.

    2.232 Exhibition of responsibility toward task performance rather than reliance on the teacher or peer reward.

2.24 Self-Direction

    2.241 Recognition of congruent and socially accepted individual goals.

    2.242 Motivation toward achieving congruent and accepted individual goals.

2.30 Values Relating to Others

2.31 Competition

    2.311 Evaluation of own present performance in comparison to own past performance.

    2.312 Evaluation of own performance in comparison to peer performance.

    2.313 Variations in goal setting relative to self and peer comparative experience.

    2.314 Acceptance of competition as a motivational device.

2.0 SOCIAL-EMOTIONAL DEVELOPMENT BEHAVIORAL EXPECTATIONS (Continued)

2.32 Cooperation

2.321 Cooperative enterprise toward self achievement.

2.322 Cooperative enterprise toward group achievement (small group to large group).

2.33 Abilities and Limitations of Others

2.331 Realization of others' abilities and limitations in comparison to oneself.

2.332 Realization of others' abilities and limitations in comparison with peer group.

2.333 Realization of others' abilities and limitations as unique to that individual.

2.34 Values and Value Systems of Others

2.341 Realization of others' values and value systems in comparison to one's own.

2.342 Realization of others' values and value systems in comparison with peer group.

2.343 Realization of others' values and value systems as unique to each individual.

2.35 Behavior of Others

2.351 Regard for the behavior of others as a guide to personal behavior.

2.352 Realization of the behavior of others as a guide to peer behavior.

2.353 Realization of self-behavior as a potential activator of others' behaviors.

2.354 Control of personal behavior as a model for peer behavior.

2.40 Concepts Regarding Groups

2.41 Variety in Group Structure

    2.411 Consideration for benefits derived for self in working with a small group.

    2.412 Consideration for benefits derived for small group.

    2.413 Consideration for members of small group.

    2.414 Consideration for changing members of small group.

    2.415 Consideration for members and changing members of ever increasing number in group.

2.42 Work in a Variety of Groups

    2.421 Awareness and communication of goals of other dyad member.

    2.422 Communication, consideration, and acceptance of goals of other member of dyad.

    2.423 Communication, awareness, consideration, and finally acceptance of alternative goals of changing group members.

    2.424 Communication of aspirations and attitudes to small and large groups.

    2.425 Communication for support to aspirations and attitudes of contributors in small and large groups.

    2.426 Congenial accord for cooperative process.

    2.427 Identity diffusion evolving to responsible identity of individual in group and his realization of individual potential.

2.50 Values Related to the Development of Humor and Empathy

    2.51 Awareness of incongruous behavior of others.

    2.52 Sensitivity to one's own incongruous behavior.

55

2.0 SOCIAL-EMOTIONAL DEVELOPMENT BEHAVIORAL EXPECTATIONS (Continued)

2.53 Sensitivity to incongruous behaviors of others.

2.54 Realization of danger/harm/derisive potential of incongruity.

2.55 Appropriate assignment of humor or compassion for incongruous behaviors in self or others.

3.0 PHYSICAL DEVELOPMENT BEHAVIORAL EXPECTATIONS
(See also 1.43, 2.12, 4.30, 4.40, 4.50, 5.20, 6.10, 6. 0)

3.10 Agility

3.11 Stop and Start

3.111 With minimum hesitation, begin a run, hop, skip, jump, other locomotor patterns from a standstill.

3.112 Terminate, with minimum hesitation any locomotor pattern without loss of balance or control.

3.12 Make rapid changes of direction in a controlled manner utilizing any locomotor pattern.

3.13 Make rapid changes from one level (low, middle, high) to another in a controlled manner while executing a locomotor pattern; change locomotor pattern while changing levels.

3.20 Balance

3.21 Static Balance

3.211 Perform one point or one patch balance: one foot, one knee, one hand, on seat, without movement of body segments or limbs (on floor, on large apparatus).

3.212 Perform one point or one patch balance with purposeful movement of body parts or segments as in twisting, rotating, swinging, squatting.

56

3.213 Perform two point balance with body inverted or upright at low, middle and high levels (on floor, on large apparatus)

3.214 Perform three point balance with body in upright or inverted position at low, middle, and high levels (on floor, on large apparatus).

3.22 Dynamic Balance

3.221 Perform locomotor patterns at varying speeds without falling or tripping.

3.222 Perform locomotor patterns combined with movements of body segments or limbs without falling or tripping.

3.223 Perform inverted locomotor skills without falling.

3.224 Combine locomotor and object handling skills and perform without falling or tripping.

3.30 Coordination

3.31 Eye-Hand

3.311 Visually follow a moving object, touch it with hand(s) and/or maintain contact with it.

3.312 Throw an object to desired location (accuracy, distance).

3.313 Strike a stationary object with hand or implement (accuracy, distance).

3.314 Strike a moving object with hand or implement (accuracy, distance).

3.315 Catch an oncoming object with one/both hands or implement.

3.32 Eye-Foot

3.321 Kick a stationary object to desired location (accuracy, distance).

3.322 Kick a moving object to desired location (accuracy, distance).

57

3.0 PHYSICAL DEVELOPMENT BEHAVIORAL EXPECTATIONS (Continued)

3.33 Speed

3.331 Decrease time between stimulus and initiation of movement with body and/or body parts (efficiency implied).

3.332 Decrease time between stimulus, initiation of movement and total movement with body and/or body parts (efficiency implied).

3.40 Endurance

3.41 Cardiovascular Endurance

3.411 Progressive stress activity to increase cardio-vascular efficiency (decreased pulse rate, faster recovery rate, decreased breathing rate) within age/development parameters.

3.412 Arrive at efficiency plateau for maintenance of work performance (maintenance of submaximal work load in sustained performance) within age/development parameters.

3.42 Muscular Endurance

3.421 Perform high intensity (maximal) tasks of short duration such as chin-ups, pushups, dashes, sprints, within age/development parameters.

3.422 Perform low intensity (submaximal) tasks of long duration such as distance running, cycling, and swimming.

3.50 Flexibility

3.51 Neck

3.511 Forward, sideward (lateral) flexion and backward extension of neck separate from shoulder girdle and trunk movements.

3.512 Rotation of head (from shoulder to shoulder) separate from shoulder girdle and trunk movements.

3.513　Forward flexion of neck in coordination with forward flexion of other body segments in specific movement activities.

3.52　Trunk

3.521　Forward, sideward flexion and backward extension of the trunk separate from movements of the pelvis.

3.522　Rotation of trunk separate from movements of pelvis.

3.523　Forward flexion of trunk in coordination with forward flexion of other body segments in specific movement activities.

3.53　Limbs

3.531　Arm raising sideward/ upward, forward/upward and backward/upward.

3.532　Rotation of arm at shoulder for full circle.

3.533　Forearm rotation.

3.534　Wrist flexion, extension, rotation.

3.535　Leg raising sideward/upward, forward/upward, backward/upward.

3.536　Knee flexion, extension, rotation.

3.537　Ankle flexion, extension, rotation.

3.54　Extremities

3.541　Extension, flexion and separation (abduction-adduction) of fingers.

3.542　Extension, flexion and separation (abduction-adduction) of toes.

3.60　Kinesthesis

3.61　Awareness of the position of body parts and body in the performance of non-locomotor and locomotor tasks.

3.0 PHYSICAL DEVELOPMENT BEHAVIORAL EXPECTATIONS (Continued)

3.62 Awareness of the position of body parts and body in the performance of object handling tasks.

3.63 Awareness of the position of body parts and the body in differing environments (land, air, water, snow, ice).

3.70 Rhythm

3.71 Self-Imposed

3.711 Perform sustained, percussive movements at own tempo with non-locomotor and locomotor movements.

3.712 Determine own rhythm pattern for performance of specific skills and tasks (running, hammering a nail, approach for a vault).

3.72 Externally Imposed

3.721 Respond to specific time signatures with non-locomotor and locomotor patterns and skills.

3.722 Respond to specific time signatures with object handling tasks.

3.723 Respond to changes in tempo maintaining a rhythm pattern with non-locomotor and locomotor patterns or skills.

3.724 Respond to changes in tempo maintaining a rhythm pattern with object handling tasks.

3.725 Perform specific dance steps and/or dances.

3.80 Strength

3.81 Sufficient arm strength to support, lift or push one's own body weight.

3.82 Sufficient leg strength to support and propel one's own body weight for daily living tasks and survival requirements.

3.83 Sufficient total body strength to meet daily living tasks and survival requirements.

3.90 Power

3.91 Combined speed and strength of arm movements to lift, push, or swing heavy objects.

3.92 Combined speed and strength of arm movements to propel body.

3.93 Combined speed and strength of leg movements to propel body in horizontal, vertical and vertical/horizontal directions.

3.94 Combined speed and strength of leg movements to propel objects.

4.0 BODY HANDLING DEVELOPMENT BEHAVIORAL EXPECTATIONS

4.10 Sensori-Motor Abilities

4.11 Body Awareness

4.111 Move arms separately, simultaneously and in alternation in purposeful movement.

4.112 Move legs separately, simultaneously and in alternation in purposeful movement.

4.113 Move arms and legs together in unilateral, bilateral and crosslateral purposeful movement.

4.114 Move body segments separately and together in purposeful movement.

4.115 Move trunk and/or arms in non-locomotor pattern while performing locomotor pattern with lower body or legs.

4.12 Body in Relation to Space

4.121 Change body shape in relation to size and shape of the space that one's body is to occupy.

61

4.0 BODY HANDLING DEVELOPMENT BEHAVIORAL EXPECTATIONS (Continued)

4.122 Select movements (non-locomotor and locomotor) appropriate to varying size and shape available for movement.

4.123 Move body with appropriate facing, at appropriate level, with appropriate locomotor pattern through variety of space types (large, small, wide, narrow, high, low, combinations of these) without over or underestimating own size in relation to the space.

4.13 Body in Relation to Surrounding Objects

4.131 Move body parts without allowing anyone or anything to touch one's body in a variety of space sizes.

4.132 Perform locomotor patterns and skills among people without bumping into them or losing own balance in variety of space sizes.

4.133 Traverse a maze or obstacle course without loss of body control.

4.134 Dodge or evade an oncoming person or object.

4.14 Discrimination

4.141 Auditory

4.1411 Move body part/body in response to beats of metronome, drum, handclaps.

4.1412 Move body/body parts in response to change in tempo.

4.1413 Move body/body parts in response to changes in tone or intensity (strong, weak, light, heavy).

4.1414 Respond with appropriate amount of force of movement to pre-assigned differing sounds (tone/kind).

4.1415 Respond with movement in appropriate direction to preassigned differing sounds (tone/kind).

62

4.1416   Respond with movement at appropriate level to preassigned differing sounds (tone/kind).

4.1417   Respond with movement at appropriate speed to preassigned differing sounds (tone/kind).

4.142 Visual

4.1421   Follow a moving light/object/person visually and indicate knowledge of it.

4.1422   Follow a moving object/person maintaining contact with it.

4.1423   Follow a moving object/person and contact it with a body part or body.

4.1424   Follow a moving object/person and avoid/evade contact of it with body part or body.

4.1425   Follow a moving object/person in a large group and contact it.

4.1426   Follow a moving object/person in a large group and evade it.

4.143 Tactile

4.1431   Utilize appropriate locomotor (walk, run, slide, etc.) movement on varying surfaces such as ice, gravel, sand, grass, gym floor.

4.1432   Make adjustments in speed and/or size of locomotor movement in relation to type of surface.

4.1433   Make adjustments in grasp (one/both hands) on object in accordance with size of object.

4.1434   Make adjustments in grasp on object in accordance with texture of object (soft, hard, rough, smooth).

4.1435   Make adjustments in grasp on object in accordance with shape of object.

4.0 BODY HANDLING DEVELOPMENT BEHAVIORAL EXPECTATIONS (Continued)

4.1436 Make adjustments in grasp on object in accordance with mass of object (heavy, light).

4.144 Kinesthetic

4.1441 Awareness of position of body parts and body in the performance of non-locomotor and locomotor tasks.

4.1442 Awareness of adjustments necessary in positioning of body/body parts as changes occur in speed, direction, force, level in performance of non-locomotor and locomotor tasks.

4.20 Non-Locomotor Patterns and Skills (Includes Body Inversion)

4.21 Functionally efficient postural control in standing, sitting, and lying (pre-action/readiness state, control state, and post performance/readiness for next action state).

4.22 Controlled non-locomotor body adjustments of preaction, in-action, and post-action required states.

4.221 Potential body performance increment via postural readiness, i.e., timing of trunk/hip rotation, torque swing (backswing).

4.222 Maintenance and control of rotatory and torque body force in execution of task (twisting, stretching, etc.).

4.30 Locomotor Patterns and Skills (Including Body Inversion)

4.31 Functional efficiency in walking, running, hopping, leaping, jumping, crawling, climbing, rolling, sliding, galloping, and skipping.

4.32 Combinatorial efficiency in multi and varied patterns and skills (run and fall, skip and leap, etc.).

4.321 Propulsion-increment of speed, power, distance variables utilizing locomotor skills.

4.322   Absorption-reduction of speed, power, distance variables utilizing locomotor skills.

4.40   <u>Combining Locomotor and Non-Locomotor Patterns and Skills</u>

4.41   Perform a locomotor pattern while performing a non-locomotor pattern with the arms (swinging, slashing, jabbing, pushing, etc.).

4.42   Perform a locomotor pattern or skill while performing a non-locomotor pattern or skill with body segments as in trunk bending/stretching, trunk rotation, head nodding, head swinging, hip swaying, etc.

4.50   <u>Combining Locomotor, Non-Locomotor and Body Awareness</u>

4.51   <u>Laterality</u>

4.511   Unilateral use of arms and legs as in bear walk, crab walk.

4.512   Unilateral use of arms and legs as in jumping jacks.

4.513   Bilateral use of arms as in hopping to increase distance or speed.

4.514   Bilateral use of arms as to assist in lift of body in two-foot take off in jumping, jumping turns, etc.

4.515   Cross-lateral use of arms and legs as in one foot takeoff in horizontal jumps, leaps.

4.52   <u>Balance</u>

4.521   Maintain balance and continuity in locomotor movement combined with bilateral non-locomotor movements as in jumping rope while on balance beam, or bouncing on a trampoline.

4.522   Maintain balance and continuity in tasks which require cross-lateral arm/leg movements.

4.60   <u>Movement Communication</u>

4.61   <u>Imitative forms as communicative, learning and teaching expressions.</u>

4.0 BODY HANDLING DEVELOPMENT BEHAVIORAL EXPECTATIONS (Continued)

4.611 Duplication of others' movements as a way of communication (people, airplanes, rabbits).

4.612 Duplication of others' movement (people, animals, things) as a process of learning.

4.613 Duplication of movements (people, animals, things) as a way to help others learn.

4.62 Expressive movements which indicate moods of performer or indicate moods of whatever performer uses them.

4.621 Utilization of movement skills and combinations of movement skills to reflect self or expression of others.

4.622 Utilization of movement skills and combinations thereof to create expression of self or others.

4.63 Interpretative movements which indicate increment in performance (speed, fluidity, etc.).

4.631 Reduce or increase parts of performance to enhance movement form or expression.

4.632 Change in movement(s) to increase function.

5.0 OBJECT HANDLING DEVELOPMENT BEHAVIORAL EXPECTATIONS

5.10 Sensori-Motor Abilities (see 4.10)

5.11 Visual pursuit accuracy displayed by proper body-readiness position (for moving object).

5.111 Perceiving oncoming objects in forward and peripheral locations at ever increasing distances.

5.112 Adjusting to readiness position with decreasing effort for visual stimuli.

5.12 Auditory perception indicated by response appropriateness.

    5.121 Attending to appropriate sounds which facilitate performance (i.e., jump rope hitting ground, noise of ball bounce, change of tempo in music).

    5.122 Responding to specific sounds by assuming readiness position with ever decreasing effort.

5.13 Tactile perception indicated by response appropriateness (shape, texture, size, weight discriminations).

    5.131 Attending to tactile cues to increase motor judgment.

    5.132 Responding to specific tactile cues, decrease reaction time, increase generalizations.

5.14 Kinesthetic perception indicated by response appropriateness: responses indicating developed kinesthetic cueing (position of body after jumping rope, etc.).

5.20 Coordination

5.21 Eye-hand perception indicated by preparation positioning, action-movement proficiency and after-movement control.

5.22 Eye-foot perception indicated by preparation positioning, action-movement proficiency and after-movement control.

5.30 Propulsion

5.31 Accuracy increments in placement of propelled object by control of eye-hand and/or eye-foot skills, incorporating force and timing.

5.32 Distance increments of propelled objects by control of eye-hand and/or eye-foot skills, incorporating timing.

5.33 Speed increments in propelling objects by control of eye-hand and/or eye-foot skills, incorporating timing.

5.0 OBJECT HANDLING DEVELOPMENT BEHAVIORAL EXPECTATIONS (Continued)

5.40 Absorption

5.41 Increments in ability to control oncoming objects (varying sizes and shapes) with the hands/feet in more demanding situations such as increased speed of oncoming object, increased distance of oncoming object, etc.

5.42 Increments in ability to control an oncoming object with an implement in the hand in more demanding situations, such as increased speed of oncoming object, increased distance of oncoming object, etc.

6.0 COORDINATED BODY AND OBJECT HANDLING DEVELOPMENT BEHAVIORAL EXPECTATIONS

6.10 Coordination

6.11 Eye-Hand-Locomotion

6.111 Increments in ability to modify timing and positioning of the body and/or hands as well as increments in visual discrimination to compensate for body momentum in the preparatory stage of movement skills (e.g., visual discrimination and timing of hand movement preparatory to passing or receiving a lummi stick in rhythm game, baton in relay race, etc.).

6.112 Same as 6.111 in the execution stage of movement skills (e.g., visual discrimination and timing of passing of stick or baton).

6.113 Same as 6.111 in the recovery stage of movement skills (e.g., visual discrimination and timing after pass in readiness for next move).

6.12 Eye-Foot-Locomotion

6.121 Increments in ability to modify timing and positioning of the body and/or feet as well as increments in visual discrimination and balance to compensate for body momentum in the preparatory stage of movement skills (e.g., visual discrimination, body positioning and timing to meet oncoming soccer ball).

68

6.122 Same as 6.121 in the execution stage of movement skills (e.g., visual discrimination and timing of swing of leg/foot positioning in stopping or kicking oncoming soccer ball.

6.123 Same as 6.121 in the recovery stage of movement skills (e.g., visual discrimination, timing and body positioning after stop or kick of ball in readiness for next move).

6.20 Propulsion of Object - Locomotion

6.21 Accuracy

6.211 Increments in accuracy of propelled objects utilizing eye-hand movement skills in translatory force (running and throwing a ball to a target).

6.212 Same as 6.211 in relation to eye-foot movement skills (running and kicking a ball to a target).

6.22 Distance

6.221 Increments in distance of propelled objects utilizing eye-hand movement skills in translatory force.

6.222 Same as 6.221 in relation to eye-foot movement skills.

6.23 Speed

6.231 Increments in speed of propelled objects utilizing eye-hand movement skills in translatory force.

6.232 Same as 6.231 in relation to eye-foot movement skills.

6.30 Object Absorption - Locomotion

6.31 Control of Body Weight

6.311 Increments in ability to make adjustments in initiation and/or slowing of body part or body movements to counteract body momentum in approaching an oncoming object.

69

6.0 COORDINATED BODY AND OBJECT HANDLING DEVELOPMENT BEHAVIORAL EXPECTATIONS (Continued)

6.312 Increments in ability to make adjustments of body and/or body parts to maintain balance when approaching an oncoming object.

6.32 Control of Object Force

6.321 Increments in ability to increase surface and/or distance to control oncoming objects.

6.322 Visual discrimination adjustments to control oncoming objects.

70

Chapter Eight
Hazelwood Behavioral Objectives
and Learning Experiences

The content of this chapter is a culmination of ideas reflected
by ten representatives of the thirty-eight physical educators in the
Hazelwood School District involved in the curriculum development project. The authors served as resources and guides to the representatives, but the views expressed by this chapter display the unique
quality and philosophy of the Hazelwood committee. The reader should
be able to find parallels in this chapter with which he can identify
and agree, and with which he cannot identify and agree. These conflicts further the argument for individualizing curriculum to particular children, groups of children, and the community which houses
them. At least, a model can be seen in these plans, and perhaps, a
theme, a purposeful direction can begin the student on the task of
organizing an ever-changing, never to be perfect set of objectives
called a curriculum.

1.0 MENTAL DEVELOPMENT

BEHAVIORAL OBJECTIVES (Student will demonstrate):	LEARNING EXPERIENCES
1.10 Knowledge and Understanding of the Human Body	
1.11 Knowledge of names and locations of body parts and segments.	1.11 Busy Bee, Keep it Moving (song), Lazy Bones, Knots.
1.12 Differentiation of body parts.	1.12 Looby Loo, Hokey Pokey, Simon Says, Back to Back, Gloves, Angels in the Snow. Set up problems asking children to use various body parts to lead them through a certain series of tasks.
1.13 Understanding of self in varying self space sizes without obstacles.	1.13 Tag games, organized dance. Problem solving (make self small).
1.14 Understanding of self in varying self space sizes with obstacles.	1.14 Hoops (over, under, through). Obstacle courses, gymnastic apparatus. Skin the snake.
1.15 Understanding of self in general spaces without obstacles.	1.15 Freeze.
1.16 Understanding of self in general spaces with obstacles.	1.16 Dodge ball, tag games, jump the shot, long and short ropes.
1.17 Understanding differences in degrees of movement at various joints (hips, shoulders, etc.).	1.17 Mirroring, stunts, problem solving involving stance, changing and movement restriction.
1.18 Understanding of various qualities of movement. a. Differences in force (strong, weak).	1.18 a. Problem solving, imitation (walk like a giant). b. Movement of a train, the talking drum.

b. Variations in time (slow, fast).
c. Variations in flow (sustained, percussive).

1.20 Movement Patterns and Skills

1.21 Pattern and Skill Terminology

1.211 Differentiation among patterns and skills: locomotor; non-locomotor; balances; object propulsion/receipt skills (put in the skills after each category).

---

c. Responding to triangle. Singing games (Wheels of the Bus, There Once Was a Teacher Who Could Not Talk).

1.211 Movement exploration: Move from one given point to another and identify how you moved. Within self space, move and identify the movement. Within self space, show how you can balance on different points and patches. From self space move given object to given point and identify how it moved. Films and records which encourage identification of movements . (Beatles go on and on and on; film loops on the patterns and skills to be identified).

Relay and tag games involving the patterns and skills to be identified. Charlie Over the Water; Brothers; Mickey Mouse; Teacher and Class; Call Ball.

Identify movement patterns and skills involved in the following: Rhythms (including balls, jump ropes, parachute) dance, folk dance and floor exercise. Dodgeball, soccer dodge-ball, mass soccer, Norwegian ball, throw and go; volleyball; soccer; floor hockey; flag football.

MENTAL DEVELOPMENT

BEHAVIORAL OBJECTIVES (Students will demonstrate a knowledge and understanding of):

LEARNING EXPERIENCES

1.212 Differentiation among movement
terms (near, far, own or self,
general), leverage, stance,
flexion (bending), extension
(stretching), backswing, follow-
through, flow (free, bound),
force, time, stop, start, change
direction.

1.212 Movement Exploration: Given certain
boundaries, see if you can find your
own space within those boundaries.
Within self space (or general space)
perform movement term to given rhythm.
Films and records which encourage
identification of the movement terms
(film loops on the movement terms to
be identified; Moving and Learning,
relay and tag games involving movement
terms, elbow tag, Red Light-Green
Light, Mother May I, bowling games
(See 1.211 exp.).

1.213 Differentiation among formations: single file, single
lines, side by side, parallel
lines, lines facing... circle,
double circle, clockwise,
counter-clockwise, square,
triangle, pairs, partners,
threes, fours... scatter.

1.213 Movement Exploration: with a group in
a given area make different formations
and identify.

Films and records which encourage
identification of formations (i.e.,
The Grand March). Games or relays
which involve any of the given formations, i.e., Mickey Mouse, Rescue
Relay, Two or Three Deep. Refer to
1.212 Experiences.

1.214 Differentiation among strategy
terms: guarding marking variations and ready positions.
(zone, double teaming, four-
point stance).

1.214 Problem solving: what is the best way
to position yourself in given games to
prevent offenses from scoring. Films
which encourage identification of
strategy terms. Relays and games
involving strategy terms: Capture the
Flag, Four Corners, One Base Kickball.
One on one, end ball, field football,

soccer, basketball, softball, track and field, flag football, wrestling.

1.215   Films encouraging identification of dance steps. Identify dance steps involved in the following rhythms (including balls, jump ropes, parachute). Creative dance, folk dance, floor exercise.

1.216   Films which encourage identification among the stunts, tumbling and gymnastic terms. Movement exploration: show different ways to move continually on four points in given area and identify how you moved. (Crab walk, bear walk, inch worm). Relays and games involving the terms to be identified; Mickey Mouse, stunt relays, follow the leader.

Identify stunts, tumbling terms in following: floor ex., free movement, use of P bars, balance beam, vaulting box, etc.

1.221   Refer to 1.211, 1.212, 1.213, 1.215, 1.216 for experiences and apply to grades three through six and explain purposes for movements.

1.222   Refer to 1.211, 1.212, 1.215, 1.216 for experiences and apply to grade levels three through six and explain purposes for movements.

1.215   Differentiation among dance steps: two step, polka, schottische, waltz, dance turns, Mazurka, Bleking, balance, dig step, grapevine.

1.216   Differentiation among stunts, tumbling and gymnastic terms; spotting, crab walk, mule kick, headstand, round-off, kip, backward hip roll, etc.

1.22   Purpose and Use of Skills

1.221   Movement and adjustments in space with or without others and/or objects; starting, stopping, changing directions, landing, side-stepping, etc...

1.222   Choice of locomotor patterns for different speeds, changes of levels and responses to specific rhythms.

BEHAVIORAL OBJECTIVES (Students will demonstrate a knowledge and understanding of):

LEARNING EXPERIENCES

1.223 Use of arms and legs
in opposition and unilaterally
with and without implements in:
throwing, hitting, receipt of
force.

1.223 Refer to 1.214 for experiences and
apply to grade levels three through
six and explain purposes for movements.

1.224 Changes of body facing with and
without implements for different types of: throwing,
hitting, receipt of force.

1.224 Refer to 1.214 (same as 1.223).

1.225 Use of bending-stretching
(fexion-extension) in propelling self and objects in
landing (receiving own weight)
and in receiving objects.

1.225 Refer to 1.211, 1.212, 1.214, 1.216
for experiences and apply for grade
levels three through six and explain
purposes for movements.

1.226 Choice of one hand or both
hands and choice of pattern
(overhand, underhand, push)
in throwing or hitting for
distance, speed, accuracy and
force; and in catching.

1.226 Refer to 1.211, 1.212 for experiences
and apply for grades three through
six and explain purposes for movements.

1.23 Pattern and Skill Continuity

1.231 Adjustment of locomotor patterns for specific tasks.

1.231 Refer to 1.214, 1.215, 1.216 for
experiences and apply. Identify
pattern and skill continuity.

1.232 Adjustment of throwing, hitting, kicking, catching for
specific tasks.

1.232 Refer to 1.211, 1.212, 1.214 for
experiences and identify pattern and
skill continuity.

1.233   Skills involving combination of body handling and object handling.

1.30 Mechanical Principles of Movement

1.31 Locomotion

1.311   The use of force production.

Refer to 1.211, 1.212, 1.214, 1.215, 1.216 for experiences and identify pattern and skill continuity.

Recognize body lean, flexion-extension, synchrony of timing, and summation of forces, in demonstrated or filmed presentations and discussions such as: Body Lean in animal walks, knee walk, running and other locomotor skills, jumps, vaults, landing. Flexion and extension in hand/arm or body part movements, exercises such as toe touches, sit-ups, locomotor skills as in skipping; sport skills as in kicking, throwing, catching in basketball, volleyball, football, soccer. Tumbling skills as in pretzels bend, forward and backward rolls, straddle rolls. Synchrony of timing in take-off and landing in jumping, run/jump combinations, serving objects... suspended, held or thrown.

1.312   The elements of stability and its maintenance during locomotion.

Problem solving: balancing on a line with one part, additional parts; lowering the center of gravity, widening the base of support in relation to type of surface, keeping center of gravity over base of support, using the arms or legs to adjust center of gravity, on all fours, as opposed to standing up straight, push partner who stands on one foot, two

MENTAL DEVELOPMENT

BEHAVIORAL OBJECTIVES (Students will demonstrate a knowledge and understanding of):

LEARNING EXPERIENCES

feet, together, 2 feet 16 inches
apart, placing feet in forward stride
position to step and change directions, raising or lowering body parts,
change levels, football stance, center
of gravity drop on Western roll, or
combatives.

1.313 Force absorption as it applies
to locomotion.

1.313 Problem solving focusing on time/
distance and chance of injury, such
as spreading shock over as large an
area as possible; when falling, or
sliding, one tries to land on a large
portion of the body. Impact absorbed
more gradually spreading shock over
as long a distance as possible (continued motion in the same direction)
for receipt of body weight. Landings as from jumps or falls. Flexion
of the joints, bending at knees, hips,
and ankles when landing from a jump.
Give more time for momentum to dissi-
pate. Control of force and momentum
(running, skipping, etc.), for stopping
with control.

1.32 Body Parts

1.321 The use of body parts in
leverage use, force production, stability, direction,
balance movements.

1.321 Discuss and/or demonstrate the increase and decrease of levers for
speed and distance such as changing
see-saw fulcrum, foot snap for rebound board, throwing with isolated
arm parts with and without a step.

Demonstrate and/or discuss the flexion and extension for force production as in stiff legged with knee bent, ankle stiff/bent kicking, walking (or other locomotion) with and without flexion of appropriate body parts.

Demonstrate and discuss flexion for stability in landing positions, scooter riding, referee's position, ready position for sports and games as fielding, basketball defense.

Demonstrate and discuss arc of swing of the leg or arm in force production and direction, kicking grounders as in passing, kicking line drives as in shooting, kicking for heights (punting). Tossing high, low, medium to self or over net, shooting basketball at varying heights.

Demonstrate and discuss flexion or extension of arms in balance as walking on floor, line, bench, beam, sitting, balance on auto tire, vaulting, combatives (Indian wrestling, slap fights), balance board skills.

1.331 Demonstrate and discuss factors such as angle of release, impact, outside forces of gravity/air currents, and synchrony of timing influencing distance, as in exploring with balls, boxes, dowel rods; tossing straws, paper plates, Frisbees, discus and shot.

1.33 Propulsion of Objects

1.331 The factors influencing propulsion of an object to the size, weight, mass and shape of the object.

MENTAL DEVELOPMENT

BEHAVIORAL OBJECTIVES (Students will demonstrate a knowledge and understanding of):

LEARNING EXPERIENCES

Demonstrate and discuss factors of
synchrony of timing, speed of lever
at time of release or impact, addition of body rotation for increased
lever length, weight transfer and
movement of body in direction of
actions (as in hitting object with
jerky movement and smooth swing)
hitting tethered and non-tethered
balls, exaggerated striking via slow
motion: ordinary speeds, scoot spin-
ning with limbs extended and con-
tracted (curled); in momentum flow
while pushing and pulling the art cart;
different size persons on scooters.

Demonstrate and discuss factors such
as angle of release, meeting of two
forces, lever direction, striking surface firmness as it influences direction such as kicking the stationary
ball with proper foot placement on
ball; batting a ball off a tee by
topping it; direct hit and under-
cutting, and changing stances to hit
inside out or outside in or pull to
right or left fields.

1.34 Receipt of Objects

1.341 The factors influencing the
       receipt of objects when catch-
       ing, body blocking, and trap-
       ping an object.

1.341 Demonstrate and discuss catching,
       blocking and trapping with bean bags,
       ball with self tossing and catching
       (use arms and body) to proper catch,

80

block or trap with "give", progressing to partner, trio or group as in hot spud, passing, relays in basketball, blocking in football, volleyball, trapping in soccer, heading or other body plays in soccer.

1.40 Physiological Factors

1.41 Differentiation between effects of health state, emotions, relaxation, stress (tension), diet, and weather on activity and performance.

Movement exploration: Move from one point to another as though you are mad, happy, sick, tense, cold, hot, etc... and identify. Discuss how these factors effect their performance during and after. Films demonstrating effects on performance (smoking, diet, emotions).

1.42 Differences in performance expectation in relation to age, weight, height and sex.

Movement exploration: Move in, around, over, under given obstacles and observe and identify differences in performance. Films demonstrating health, the differences in relation to age, weight, height and sex. Also performance films of different age groups playing sports, swimming, etc... discuss differences.

1.43 Effects of exercise on heart rate, breathing, muscle tone, general feeling of well being.

Take pulse rate and observe breathing after strenuous activity in comparison with after a relaxation period (place hand over heart, place fingers at neck). Compare results of physical fitness type testing given at different times during the school year.

1.44 Increase in number and/or intensity to build strength and endurance.

Refer to 3.40 and 3.80 for ideas and discuss.

81

MENTAL DEVELOPMENT

BEHAVIORAL OBJECTIVES (Students will demonstrate a knowledge and understanding of):	LEARNING EXPERIENCES
1.45 Increase of range of movement at joints by increased stretching to gain greater flexibility.	1.45 Refer to 3.50 and discuss.
1.46 Fitness level increases with activity and decreases with inactivity.	1.46 Comparison of ability to perform fitness activities after vigorous activities in comparison with ability to perform fitness activities after less vigorous activities.
1.47 The importance of "warming up" and "cooling down" body parts before and then after vigorous activity.	1.47 Discussion and trials of warming up and cooling down: bending, stretching activities before running low hurdles; walking around after long run instead of sitting down.
1.50 Rules and Strategies	
1.51 Rules and Regulations for Specific Activities	
1.511 The need to share space with others and to respect the space of others.	1.511 Exploration of various sized spaces with varying group sizes in performing locomotor activities, games, dances, etc.
	Discussion of results of ignoring others while moving in above situations.
1.512 The correct use of specific equipment.	1.512 Discuss the reasons specific hand equipment (volleyballs, softballs, tennis balls, soccer balls, etc.) is to be kicked, thrown, or hit.

82

1.513 The appropriateness of specific activities performed in specific areas and on specific equipment.

Experiment (where equipment will not be damaged) with other uses than that for which designed.

Incorporate information from 1.33 and 1.53.

1.513 Discussion and experimentation with activities in specified areas and on specific equipment to determine appropriateness of activities.

1.514 The rules of specific games or other activities.

1.514 Discussion of rules and participation in specific activities from 4.0, 5.0, and 6.0 - utilizing these rules.

1.52 Strategies for Specific Activities

1.521 Working by oneself in specific activities such as throwing to self, rebounding objects, achieving height, distance, and accuracy.

1.521 Bean bag self toss, ball toss against wall, scoop/throw ball against wall, basketball jump shot and one-hand push shot.

1.522 Working with a partner in specific activities such as: couple stunts, ball passing, combatives, tether ball, rope jumping, rhythmic activities (lummi sticks, partner dances).

1.522 Toe boxing, club take down, thumb wrestle, tether ball, partner rope turning/jumping, lummi sticks, leapfrog, partner hopping, twister, wring the dish rag, churn the butter, Chinese get-up, double scooter, Eskimo roll, ball passing with partner, LaRaspa, Kinderpolka.

1.523 Working in small groups in specific activities such as: passing objects, evading opponents, achieving ready positions, pyramid building, performing rhythmic activities

1.523 Hot potato, over-under relay, Danish rounders, beat the ball, baton relay, sport ready position, stop and out, dodge ball, exchange dodge ball, pyramid building, tinikling, ball, hoop and rope routines, Seven jumps.

BEHAVIORAL OBJECTIVES (Students will demonstrate a knowledge and understanding of):	LEARNING EXPERIENCES
(tinikling, folk dancing, ball/hoop/rope routines).	
1.524 Specific movement activities with large groups.	1.524 Discussion of games, relays, gymnastics, dances, midnight, Cowboys and Indians, fishes and whales, Paw Paw Patch, Farmer in the Dell, Virginia reel.
1.53 Safety Factors	
1.531 Hazard of hitting, throwing object, of running through area where groups are performing another activity.	1.531 Discussion of hazards through skits.
1.532 Improper use of equipment and horse play or laughing while performing activities on apparatus and large equipment, or while others are performing activities.	1.532 Demonstrate, discuss hazards and illustrate through skits.
1.533 The need to determine rules to avoid injury and/or equipment damage in above situations.	1.533 Have students participate in group discussion forming necessary rules for safety on equipment or during activity.
1.60 Common Related Concepts	
1.61 Art	
1.611 Realization of body parts and total body form as similar to	1.611 "Like a" mimetic activities (animals, objects, cartoon characters).

all forms and structures within nature.

1.612 Awareness of movement as a depth dimension of form and structure.

Activities involving use of circles, squares, rectangles. (Hoops, boxes, balls). Whale drawings upon which to walk, leap, etc.

1.612 Visually track an object coming toward and going from student and discuss perceptual changes of size of that object. Crepe paper streamers used to create visual blurs. (See 1.613).

1.613 Awareness of color and intensity as compatible factors in flow and movement.

1.613 Creating visual blurs of colors by using crepe paper streamers. Hot colors-cold colors game using color intensity as cueing devices. Strong weak colors and forms games. (Blocks are strong, playing cards are weak). Relate quality of movement in movement exploration activities.

1.614 Aesthetic concepts in movement.

1.614 Student will replicate position/movement as portrayed in art works (use overhead projector). Student moves in ways that are strong, kind, pensive, etc. (creative movement forms).

1.615 Identification with the world of art through increasing appreciation of movement and concepts gained thereby.

1.615 Refer to experiences in 1.611 thru 1.614.

1.62 Language Arts

1.621 Communication of movement experiences (oral and written) for self and others.

1.621 "Show and tell" using movement to describe (partner and small group). Play follow the leader having leader write commands for followers. Express orally what has been done in movement.

85

MENTAL DEVELOPMENT

BEHAVIORAL OBJECTIVES (Students will demonstrate a knowledge and understanding of):

	BEHAVIORAL OBJECTIVES	LEARNING EXPERIENCES
1.622	Interpretation of communication into movement forms and experiences (to know what to do from what is said or read).	Task cards with written directions for various stations. For younger children, use task cards with captions at the base of visuals. Simon says, Hokey Pokey, Chicken Fat.
1.623	Realization of the great need for syntactic and semantic abilities in learning, performing, and planning movement experiences.	Small group activities (pyramids, organized obstacle courses with specific equipment). Activities which demand the children communicate to arrive at goal. Have students help partners to accomplish written task.
1.624	Documentation (written evidence) of one's own movement performance and experiences.	Record in acceptable written form the results of one's own movement experiences. Write a creative composition in dance, gymnastics, game strategy (after having performed same).

1.63 Math

1.631	Sets: the similarities and dissimilarities of those characteristics of movement and the beings that are able to move.	Using a parachute, have children release and cross under the chute to new positions if they are wearing/own/have: blue sneakers, glasses, dungarees, belt buckles, brown hair, dogs, goldfish, cats, etc. (Steal the bacon using same concept). Mirrors. Follow the Leader.
1.632	Priorities in difficulties and degrees of movement and the changing orders through movement experiences.	Have children trace partners' forms on food market bags and display on wall in order of height. Have students aware of the whys of gymnastic

progressions. Post in gym and have student note.

1.633 Have students record performances in track and field, basketball skills, etc. Count and record and maintain records as math practice and evidence of performance increments.

1.634 Counting while rope jumping, ball bouncing, and any activity where possible to serve as motivational device. In higher grades, to understand maximum power can be achieved from 45° angle ready position (broad jump, spring start, distance throws) and to work to kinesthetic awareness reflecting that and related principles.

1.635 Have student translate movement activities into symbol forms of mathematics relative to description of distances, spaces, times, forces and to translate from math symbol description to movement expression.

1.641 Have student clap, walk, run, etc. to rhythm of music. Pairs of students lead and follow partner's rhythm. Rhythm bands (bottle cap tamborines, coffee tins, pots, etc.). Replicate rhythm patterns in specific design patterns.

1.642 Have student begin, continue, and finish a goal oriented movement task to music and without music. Discuss

1.633 Measurement and records of personal movement experience using math codes.

1.634 Use of math to aid in learning, performing and planning movement experiences.

1.635 Movement as a basis for the understanding of distance, space, time, force, and that the symbol system representing movement is the substance of mathematics.

1.64 Music

1.641 Rhythm as evidence of movement experience. Sound is made in movement and can be monitored and replicated in movement(s) with timing similarities.

1.642 Melody as the content of movement events gives meaning to a movement composition. Awareness that

MENTAL DEVELOPMENT

BEHAVIORAL OBJECTIVES (Students will demonstrate a knowledge and understanding of):	LEARNING EXPERIENCES
music is compatible to movement performance.	parallel components of movement task composition and melodic composition. Experience various melodic compositions and apply to movement tasks. Specific dances and forms.
1.643 Utilization of music and the components of music for the purpose of learning, performing, and planning movement experiences.	1.643 Have student experience learning a movement task, the rhythm of which is replicated in musical composition. (Use music to "practice by"). Plan a movement performance to a specific piece of music (basketball passing drill or bouncing drill). Have student replicate rhythm of a particular task and add to other movement tasks in sequence.
1.644 Appreciation of music as sound illustrated documents of movement and time.	1.644 All of 1.635, 1.641, 1.642 and 1.643 Learning Experiences.
1.65 Science	
1.651 Utilization of mathematic and communication codes to describe the scientific aspects of movement experiences.	1.651 All of 1.62 and 1.63 Learning Experiences.
1.652 The natural boundaries described by science that delineate the possibilities of human movement experiences.	1.652 Have student experiment with maximum performance individually/partner and small groups. Establish reason for limitations and relate to physical laws.

88

1.653   "Timber" on the mats, centripetal and centrifugal force activities (line tag), transfer of momentum activities (side by side by side reactions). Trampoline utilization in rebound tumbling. Discuss principles.

1.654   See 1.30 activities.

1.655   See 1.30 activities.

1.66   See 2.0 Learning Experiences for all 1.66 entries.

1.653   Realization of human movement experience as a predicator of science phenomena; to relate movement experience to possible events in nature.

1.654   Employment of physical laws in learning, performing and planning human movement experiences.

1.655   The physical properties and laws of nature are inseparable from the properties and laws concerning and governing the human body and the movement of the human body.

1.66   Social Science

1.661   Realization of self values by seeing the values of others displayed in human movement experiences.

1.662   Control of self and others for the purpose of individual and coactors achievement.

1.663   Realization of self as leader or follower and appropriateness of role as event/experience/group members dictate.

1.664   Realization of group structures as a learning, performing, and planning consideration in human movement experience.

89

MENTAL DEVELOPMENT

BEHAVIORAL OBJECTIVES (Students will demonstrate):	LEARNING EXPERIENCES
1.665 The social opportunities presented in a P.E. experience provide an open-ended forum for the understanding of one's self and others. Governance and achievement are relative to co-action movement experience.	

2.0 SOCIAL-EMOTIONAL DEVELOPMENT

2.10 Appreciation & Acceptance of Physical Activity

2.11 Enjoyment in Physical Endeavor

2.111 Appreciation as a spectator: of peer performance and skilled performers in various psycho-motor events.	2.111 Films; demonstrations (by peers and performers); field trips to watch performers; television (i.e. Wide World of Sports).
2.112 Enjoyment in participation in established and novel psycho-motor events.	2.112 Encourage organized individualized freeplay - discourage competition; perform skills, games and activities adjusted to students' ability levels. See 4.0 and 5.0 Learning Experiences.

2.12 Effects of Physical Activity

2.121 An awareness of beneficial physiological effects of movement activity participation.	2.121 Refer to 1.40 and discuss.

2.122 An awareness of movement activity participation as an avenue to socialization (partner, group, teams).

2.122 Discussion of what is learned by playing with others in different game types situations (i.e. sportsmanship, cooperation, etc.). Films involving social-emotional aspects of play and team work, discuss; Pictures demonstrating social-emotional aspects, discuss; Pointing out problems encountered during actual game situations, discuss.

2.123 An awareness of the role of movement activity participation as a vent for and/or alleviator of emotional tensions (sublimation potential).

2.123 Discuss what happens when feelings rise (i.e., anger, frustration, excitement) and what they usually do to get rid of these feelings. Then discuss possibilities for participation in game types of activities or physical activities to relieve such emotions.

2.124 An awareness of movement activity participation as an avenue for self-expression and self-realization.

2.124 Movement exploration where movement is not directed toward a specific goal. Allowing free play with various objects and obstacles encouraging new and expressive games or experiences (i.e., place several different objects in a group and allow students to invent new game).

2.13 Participation in Movement Activities

2.131 A willingness to participate in movement activities to derive pleasure, to realize socialization potential (partner, group, team) and to realize creative potential.

2.131 Refer to 2.114 for learning experiences. Organized free play encouraging the objectives. Individual, partner and group activities encouraging creative skill development. (From simple activities to highly organized activities - see 2.14).

SOCIAL-EMOTIONAL DEVELOPMENT

BEHAVIORAL OBJECTIVES (Students will demonstrate):

LEARNING EXPERIENCES

2.132 A willingness to participate in movement activities to derive physiological benefits (cardio-respiratory/skeleto-muscular fitness).

2.132 Refer to 1.40. Organized free play encouraging running, tag games, rope jumping, climbing (monkey bars, jungle gym), highly organized games, folk dance, gymnastics, swimming, etc.

2.14 Achievement of Skill and Success in Movement Activities

2.141 Establishment of realistic achievable goals for all movement activity participation.

2.141 Films showing skill level they have been through and can achieve in different areas (stunts and tumbling, creative dance, rope jumping, etc....). Refer to 2.111. Keep individual records on skills achieved in any given area. Post outstanding records on given skills to encourage increased goals.

2.142 Maintenance of a positive level of aspiration within a realistic scope of his or her abilities.

2.142 Refer to 2.131 Learning Experiences so that students will be encouraged to continue increasing their goals (in reference to moving up to organized sports and more competitive activities).

2.15 Non-Verbal Communication Through Movement

2.151 Recognition of movement as a form of communication of feelings, mood, emotion, attitudes from self to others and from others to self.

2.151 Refer to 4.62 and have students watch each other perform and then discuss.

92

2.152 Recognize movement as a form of
communication of ideas from simple
gestures and postures to sophisti-
cated choreography.

2.152 Refer to 4.611 and have students
watch each other perform and then
discuss.

2.20 Values of a Positive Self-Concept

2.21 Recognition and acceptance of own
abilities and limitations and willingness to make adjustments for
them.

2.21 Explain the criteria needed for each
activity such as rope climbing, dance,
tumbling. Provide a variety of self-
testing activities and have student
determine his status of performance of
them.

Have student choose a partner of his
own skill level. Have students form
a group of equal skill ability for
specific activity participation, e.g.,
combatives, partner and group stunts,
basketball one on one, etc... Encourage student to perform all skills
to the best of his ability (standing
on head as long as possible, doing
mule kick instead of hand stand) and
note that his peers perform some things
better than they do others, just as he
performs some things better than he
performs other activities.

2.22 Body image awareness of his own
body structure and growth as it
pertains to his performance.

2.22 Have student judge body size by
marking partner's height, width, body
part size on floor or wall. Directing
self and others into different sizes
and shapes. Set up obstacle course
and include small, narrow, large, high,
low spaces to go through and under.
Have student choose partner of equal
size for combatives. Have students
determine most suitable position for

93

SOCIAL-EMOTIONAL DEVELOPMENT

BEHAVIORAL OBJECTIVES (Students will demonstrate):	LEARNING EXPERIENCES
	self and for other teammates in a team game (football, basketball, gymnastics, etc...).
2.23 Self-discipline awareness of his own behavior and acceptance of responsibility for it.	2.23 Set up situation where children are responsible for returning equipment at stations before moving to next activity. Set up tag game or simple game in which student must monitor own performance (admit when tagged, score number of goals made, etc.).
	Set stations with task cards with student responsibility for recording tasks completed by group members. Use student officials for games, timing track events, etc.. Discuss acceptance of peer decisions if situation arises in above items.
2.24 Self-direction. Recognition of congruent and socially acceptable goals and willingness to strive for them.	2.24 Have children form groups of 2 - 4 in size and have them work individually on tasks they will need to use in a larger group activity. Tasks should be challenging and enjoyable. Set up stations with task variety within scope of all students - have students select tasks at stations within own ability limits.
	Have students set up goals for individual behavior in light of criteria for successful participation in the activities. Discuss (at end of class) how many criteria were met.

2.30 Values Relating to Others

2.31 Competition

2.311	Willingness to evaluate own present performance in comparison to own past performance.	Refer to 2.131 on individual records. Self-evaluation in movement activities (i.e., walking balance beam entire distance without falling, bouncing ball x number of times without stopping, timing self on distance running, maintaining control of soccer ball for given distance and course).
2.312	Willingness to evaluate own performance in comparison to peer performance.	Refer to 2.131 (posted records). Observe others performance and help others evaluate selves on different movement activities.
2.313	Willingness to set various goals relative to self and peer comparative experiences.	Refer to 2.311 and 2.312 and discuss with students so that he or she may evaluate for self.
2.314	Acceptance of competition as a motivational device.	Refer to 2.311, 2.312 and 2.313 and discuss how the evaluation and comparison has motivated or not motivated them to continue to achieve and set higher goals.

2.32 Cooperation

2.321	Cooperation with others while working toward self-achievement.	Have students perform partner activities which involve cooperation. Then discuss how working together can help each student. Advance to larger group activities which involve more cooperation and discuss again; (ball bounce, catch partner activity to games such as tadpole and then on to team sports).

SOCIAL-EMOTIONAL DEVELOPMENT

LEARNING EXPERIENCES

BEHAVIORAL OBJECTIVES (Students will demonstrate):

2.322 Cooperation with others while working toward group-achievement.

2.322 Refer to 2.321 and apply to group goals (small to large groups) for different games and skill drills.

2.33 Abilities and Limitations of Others

2.331 Recognition of other's abilities and limitations in comparison to oneself and peer group.

2.331 Refer to 1.41, 1.42, 2.131, 2.132, 2.311, 2.312, 2.313 and 3.0 generally.

Films dealing with individual differences (handicapped, dwarfs and types of bodies).

Discussion of why people are different and how differences affect performance. Then point out differences of students in class which cannot embarrass the students involved (tallness and shortness, how glasses affect performance and must be removed to perform certain activities).

2.332 Recognition of others' abilities and limitations as unique to each individual.

2.332 Refer to 2.331 Learning Experiences and continue discussion as to how their abilities and limitations are their own and they must learn to adjust to them.

2.34 Values and Value Systems of Others

2.341 Recognition of others' values and value systems in comparison to one's own and with the peer group.

2.341 Films dealing with honesty, sharing, sportsmanship, etc. Discussion of the values seen on film and encountered in class situations.

2.342 Recognition of values and value systems as unique to each individual.

2.342 Refer to 2.341 and discuss how each person has different values and how some values will be the same and the significance of these values.

Have students referee their own games as a group and individually. Encourage students to settle their own arguments through verbal communication. Use student arbitrators to improve communication in arguments.

2.35 Awareness of Behavior of Others

2.351 Recognition of the behavior of others as a guide to personal and peer behavior.

2.351 Refer to 2.31, 2.32, 2.33 and 2.34 Learning Experiences and discuss.

2.352 Control of personal behavior as a potential activator for others as well as a model for behavior of peers and others.

2.352 Refer to 2.31, 2.32, 2.33 and 2.34 Learning Experiences and discuss. Emphasize control.

2.40 Concepts Regarding Groups

2.41 Recognition and acceptance of the advantages and disadvantages of changing group size and/or structure.

2.41 Set up situations where objects are gathered under time limit by oneself and then by small groups, then larger groups.

Problem solving with group: building bridges with objects, making geometric designs with group, pyramids and partner stunts.

SOCIAL-EMOTIONAL DEVELOPMENT

BEHAVIORAL OBJECTIVES (Students
will demonstrate):

LEARNING EXPERIENCES

Team games and sports with varying
numbers of participants.

2.42 Work in variety of groups and the
ability to communicate goals of
other group members, to accept
changing membership in a group,
and changing goals, and to cooperate as a contributing member.

2.42 Follow your partner, mirroring, then
do the same activity changing the
leadership (follow the leader, Simon
says). Square and folk and creative
dance.

Have group create own game, dance,
stunt routine with change of group
members in accordance with skill needs
of the activity. As the situation
arises in above (or set up situation),
discuss aspects of acceptance of others
and/or goals in realizing success in
particular endeavor for group and each
group member.

2.50 Values related to the development
of humor and empathy.

Recognition and appreciation of
humor, the humor in incongruous
behavior, and be empathetic with
this behavior in self and others.

2.50 Discuss meaning of incongruous behavior and have students point out
humor of specific incongruous behavior occurrences. Discuss appropriate assignment of humor or compassion for incongruous behaviors in
self or others.

98

3.0 PHYSICAL DEVELOPMENT

3.10 Agility

3.11 Starting from a standstill and stopping on signals with little hesitation and without losing control of the following loco- motor skills: roll, crawl, walk, run, hop, jump, slide, gallop, skip, leap.

3.11 Start and stop to a signal, verbal and non-verbal.

Fleeing, chasing, dodging, singing games and rhythm games, (Seven Jumps, Looby Loo).

3.12 Locomotor skills (as in 3.11) in varying directions quickly.

3.12 Move up, down, forward, backward, sideward, clockwise, combination of directions, with turns, zig zag, changing patterns, pivoting, cutting (football), feinting, shuttle run, relays.

3.13 Locomotor skills with control and rapidity on varying levels.

3.13 Problem solving evolving to command response: jumping, vaulting, spring up, kip, diving forward roll, monkey roll, blocking (football), goalie skills (hockey, soccer). Sprint starts.

3.14 Changing locomotor patterns while changing levels with control.

3.14 Walk into a gorilla walk, problem solving with choice of patterns and levels, run into a forward dive roll.

3.20 Balance

3.21 Static Balance

3.211 A one point balance on either foot, knee, or seat without moving body parts.

3.211 Balance on either foot, balance on one foot for 5 seconds, balance on either foot on a line, balance on low balance beam, stork stand on either foot, toe to knee

BEHAVIORAL OBJECTIVES (Students will demonstrate):

LEARNING EXPERIENCES

balance on either foot, arabesque, using apparatus or equipment. Balance on either knee on mat, balance on either knee for 5 seconds, balance on knee on different surfaces, floor, bean bag, etc.

Balance on seat with knees bent, balance with one knee bent, one straight, balance with legs straight at different heights from floor, V-seat on floor, V-seat using different equipment or apparatus.

3.212 A one point balance on one foot, knee, or seat while twisting, swinging, rotating, bending, stretching or other suitable axial non-locomotor movements.

3.212 Balance on one foot, knee, or seat twisting trunk, balance on line while twisting trunk using equipment or apparatus.

Balance on one foot, knee or seat rotating head left then right, balance rotating trunk left and right, balance rotating arms, do same on apparatus or with equipment.

Balance on one foot, one knee, or seat swinging one arm; balance swinging one leg, balance swinging head, use swinging activities on apparatus or with equipment.

Balance on one foot, one knee, or seat stretching arms, bending arms, stretching and bending trunk while balanced. Stretching or bending one leg while balanced, use stretching and bending in balanced position on apparatus or with equipment.

Balance on one foot and squat on the floor, balance on one line and squat, do same using equipment and apparatus.

3.213 Do all of the above activities using mimetics such as throwing, catching, swimming, hammering, etc. Also use with equipment and apparatus for these balance activities.

3.214 Stand on line, stand on apparatus or equipment, squat on line, squat on apparatus or equipment, balance on toes, balance on toes for 10 seconds, balance on toes on apparatus or equipment, knee scale on floor, knee scale on line, knee scale on apparatus or equipment.

3.215 Tip up or frog stand on floor, tip up or frog stand on equipment, hand stand assisted, hand stand unassisted on floor, hand stand on apparatus assisted, hand stand unassisted using apparatus or equipment, forearm stand on floor.

3.216 Do all of the above activities using non-locomotor movements or mimetics.

3.213 A one point balance on one foot, knee or seat while performing mimetics.

3.214 A two point balance in an upright position using high, medium and low levels.

3.215 A two point balance in an inverted position.

3.216 A two point balance using non-locomotor movements or mimetics.

PHYSICAL DEVELOPMENT

BEHAVIORAL OBJECTIVES (Students
will demonstrate):

LEARNING EXPERIENCES

3.217 A three point balance with body in
       upright or inverted position,
       using low, medium and high levels.

3.217 Upright:
       Balance on two hands and one foot,
       balance on two feet and one hand on
       floor, repeat using apparatus and
       equipment, balanced V-seat on equip-
       ment and apparatus.

       Inverted:
       Tripod, head stand, head stand from
       pike position, head stand with legs
       split, head stand with legs bent and
       the other straight, forearm head
       stand on floor.

3.218 A three point balance in upright
       or inverted position performing
       non-locomotor movements and
       mimetics.

3.218 Do all above activities using non-
       locomotor movements or mimetics.

3.219 A one, two, or three point
       balance while balancing
       objects.

3.219 Do all of the above activities bal-
       ancing bean bags, wands, balls,
       hoops, scoops, cylinders, Indian
       clubs, ropes and rings, etc.

3.22   Dynamic Balance

3.22   *Mimetic to exploration to specific
       response to creative composition.
       (Progress slow to fast).

*In all Dynamic Balance Learning Experiences

102

3.221 Locomotor skills such as rolling,
       crawling, walking, running, slid-
       ing, hopping, jumping, galloping,
       leaping, and skipping at varying
       speeds with control.

3.221 Rolling in varying body positions
       and directions such as log roll, egg
       roll, human ball.

       Crawl forward shifting weight, crawl
       backward, crawl under obstacle, crawl
       sideward, crawl on bench.

       Walk forward, backward, sideward,
       zig-zag; on the floor, on a rope, a
       line, and a bench, a beam or other
       equipment using control and proper
       form.

       Running forward, backward, sideward,
       and zig-zag using various floor shapes
       and patterns such as circles, squares,
       triangles, etc.

       Running forward, backward, sideward,
       and zig-zag using various floor
       shapes and patterns such as circles,
       squares, triangles, etc.

       Running patterns used in low orga-
       nized games such as chasing and flee-
       ing, running with a partner, etc.

       Running patterns used in sports
       activities such as base running,
       football patterns, etc.

       Slide right, slide left, slide in
       varying designs, slide with partners.
       Slide in game situations such as toy
       chase, basketball (defense), etc.

PHYSICAL DEVELOPMENT

LEARNING EXPERIENCES

Hopping on right, on left; in varying
directions, designs, and patterns,
hopping over, in, and on objects
(tires).

Jumping forward, backward, sideward,
zig-zag, using various designs;
jumping on, over, in, and through
objects, jumping in game situations,
standing long jump.

Galloping forward, backward, to the
right and left, in various designs.
Galloping in low organized games such
as cut the cake, cat and rat, etc.
Galloping in lead-up games such as
one base, etc.

Leaping forward, backward, and sideward; over objects, in objects, and
on objects; in low organized games
such as brothers, relays, running
long jump.

Skipping forward and backward; in
different directions and patterns;
on objects, in objects, and over
objects; in relays, low-organized
games and lead up games.

3.222   Arms overhead, to one side, to either
        side, and to opposite side, at sides,
        forward and backward. Repeat with
        legs.

3.222   The above locomotor skills in
        combination with body segment
        and limb movement with control.

104

Head forward, backward, sideward, swinging, rotating or shaking. Trunk move in any direction such as forward, backward, or around. Axial movements such as bending, twisting, etc. Using hands, fingers, elbows, toes, feet and shoulders. Use any feasible combination of the above activities such as elephant, seal, crab, bear, lame dog, and other walks.

3.223   The previous listed locomotor skills with control while handling objects.

Do all of the previous listed activities using the appropriate objects; bean bags, balls, hoops, wands, or sticks, rings, cylinders, ropes, parachute and Indian clubs.

3.224   Inverted locomotor skills without falling.

Walking arch up or bridge, forward roll progression, backward roll progression, fish flop, cartwheel, round off, walking on hands, front walk over, back walk over, tinsica, head springs, and hand springs.

3.225   Inverted locomotor and object handling skills with control.

Do the above listed activities (3.224) using the listed objects in Section 3.223.

3.30   Coordination

3.31   Eye-hand Coordination

3.311   Visually track a moving object by touching it with hand(s) and/or maintain contact with it.

Touch suspended moving ball on string, tracking Frisbee, balloon, leaf, or feather in flight with finger, shadow tag games.

PHYSICAL DEVELOPMENT

BEHAVIORAL OBJECTIVES (Students
will be able to):

LEARNING EXPERIENCES

3.312 Catch an object with one or both
hands or implement.

3.312 Bean bags and balls...i.e., utility
balls, yarn balls, Nerf and tennis
balls used in the following ways:
toss and catch to self; toss and
catch with one hand; toss-clap-catch.
Use above activities with locomotor
skills. Figure "8" around knees.
Catch object rebounding from a given
surface, i.e., floor, wall.

Catch and step with partner. Catching
a batted or kicked ball.

Implements - scoops, gloves, etc.
See bean bag and ball activities for
ideas. Low organized games: involving catching, i.e., Circle Call Ball,
Spud, Nervous Wreck.

Lead Ups...Bombardment, Newcomb,
Kickball.

Team sports...softball, flag football.

3.313 Throw an object to a desired
stationary location for desired
accuracy and distance.

3.313 Stationary target games using throw-
able objects thrown at varied sizes
of targets using varied distances,
i.e.,...clown face target, hoops,
waste baskets, etc.

Low organized games - Guard the
Castle, Pin Bombardment, Line Roll
Ball, Throw and Go.

106

Lead-Up games - End ball, field football.

Team sports - basketball, speedball field events (softball throw).

3.314 Throw an object to a desired moving location for desired accuracy and/or distance.

Moving target games using varied sizes of targets at varied distances, i.e....suspended tire, rolling hoop, etc.

Low organized games - Roll Dodge Ball, Shoot the Rapids, etc.

Lead-Up games - Boundary ball, end zone.

Team sports - flag football, speedball, softball, kickball.

3.315 Strike a stationary object with hand or implement for accuracy and/or distance.

Strike Stationary Hanging Object (Suspended Wiffle Ball).
Strike object from atop a cone or other supports, (fat bat, hand).

Low organized games - Involving Striking, Punch ball, Tee Ball.

Team sports - involving striking, volleyball, underhand serve.

3.316 Strike a moving object with hand or implement for accuracy and/or distance.

Yarn Ball Striking (Bladder Volleyball) balloon tapping. Striking moving hanging object (suspended). Wiffle ball (hit/stick).

Paddle - Strike ball on paddle - strike ball against given surface.

BEHAVIORAL OBJECTIVES (Students will be able to):

LEARNING EXPERIENCES

Strike ball on paddle turning paddle each time.

Bat - strike tossed ball.

Hockey stick - strike puck.

Triangle ball, softball, hockey, scooter hockey.

3.32 Eye-Foot

3.321 Kick a stationary object to a desired location for accuracy and/or distance.

3.321 Problem solving i.e., how hard (easy) must you kick to reach desired destination. Stationary kick of stationary object. Step kick of stationary object. Series of steps to kick stationary object. Use above kicks with different foot surface i.e., instep kick, infield ball kicking, kickball, Danish rounder, sports involving kicking: soccer, football, speedball.

3.322 Kick a moving object to desired location for accuracy and/or distance.

3.322 Problem solving approach, i.e., how hard (easy) must you kick to reach desired destination.

While stationary, kick moving ball.

Step kick a moving ball. Series of steps to kick moving ball.

Use above kicks with different foot surfaces - i.e., instep kick. Do above emphasizing ball control.

Low organized games - involving kicking. Use 3.321 games using rolled ball to kicker. Kick out.

Lead-Up games - Kickball, line soccer, crab soccer.

Team sports - involving kicking: soccer, kickball, football (punt), speedball.

3.33 Speed

3.331 Ability to decrease time between stimulus and initiation of movement with body and/or body parts, efficiency implied.

3.331 Problem solving i.e., Stop/Start on signal (sound or sight command) using all locomotor movements. Start on whistle, stop on whistle. Combination sight/sound stimulus i.e., start on whistle, stop at given line.

Use all of above with combination of non-locomotor and locomotor skills.

3.332 Decrease time between stimulus, initiation of movement and total movement with body and/or body parts, efficiency implied.

3.332 Use above learning experiences with Objectives 3.312 - 3.322.

Freeze Tag, Nervous Wreck, Circle Stride Ball.
Pepper, Basketball, Faking.
Sport Softball, Basketball, Creative Dance.

3.40 Endurance

3.41 Cardiovascular Endurance

PHYSICAL DEVELOPMENT

BEHAVIORAL OBJECTIVES (Students will be able to):

LEARNING EXPERIENCES

3.411 Perform progressive stress activity to increase cardiovascular efficiency (decreased pulse rate, faster recovery rate, decreased breathing rate) within age development parameters.

3.411 Use activities that reduce stress, i.e., walking in place and moving, marching tortoise and hare (in place and moving), run and jump, jump-nastics, rope jumping, running-sprints or dashes, endurance runs.

Circuit training.

Partner Timing Recovery Rate - Refer to Mental 1.40.

3.412 Arrive at efficiency plateau for maintenance of work performance (maintenance of submaximal work load in sustained performance) within age/development parameters.

3.412 Using 3.411 experiences, increase number, decrease time and/or increase distance.

3.42 Muscular Endurance

3.421 Perform intensity (maximal) tasks of short duration within age/development parameters.

3.421 Stunts - seal walk, seal walk with clap, walrus walk, mule kick, kip-up, climbing parallel cargo net, 50 yard dash (increase distance) rope climbing, push ups, chin ups, leaps, long jumps.

Low organized games - Mickey Mouse, relays-gymnastics activities i.e., vaulting, balance beam mounts, dismounts, floor exercise.

	Objective	Activities/Examples
3.422	Perform low intensity (submaximal) tasks of long duration within age/development parameters.	Swing from rope and horizontal bar and rings, flexed arm hang. Endurance running (600 yard run). Gymnastics activities i.e., floor exercise, parallel bars, etc.

3.50 Flexibility

3.51 Neck

	Objective	Activities/Examples
3.511	Perform forward, sideward (lateral) flexion and backward extension of neck separate from shoulder girdle and trunk movements.	Chicken pecks, neck nod, Egyptian neck bobs.
3.512	Rotate head (shoulder to shoulder) separate from shoulder girdle and trunk movements	Head circles, refer to Tracking Activities 3.311 and use nose instead of finger without contact.
3.513	Forward flexion of neck in coordination with forward flexion of other body segments in specific movement activities.	Problem solving, i.e., making self into ball using different points and patches, curling into small spaces, making body into shapes and letters. Tripod, forward roll, back rocker, bicycle, backward roll, headstand, forearm stand, neck bridge.

3.52 Trunk

	Objective	Activities/Examples
3.521	Forward, sideward flexion and backward extension of the trunk separate from movements of the pelvis.	Trunk sway (side), wall trunk sway (backward, forward), toe touches, butterfly lift.
3.522	Rotate the trunk separate from movements of pelvis.	Trunk twister, bumps, grinds.

PHYSICAL DEVELOPMENT

BEHAVIORAL OBJECTIVES (Students will be able to):

LEARNING EXPERIENCES

3.523 Forward flexion of trunk in co-ordination with forward flexion of other body segments in specific movement activities.

3.523 Twister, sit-ups, bowling/rolling, throwing, cartwheels, roundoffs, handsprings, aerial gymnastic activities on bars and rings, i.e., Skin the Cat, etc.

3.53 Limbs

3.531 Raise arms sideward/upward, forward/upward and backward/upward.

3.531 Movement exploration, i.e., ways to move arms (how wide, how tall, etc.), jumpnastics, parachute, umbrella, mushroom, mountain, isometrics, bicep builder, cross arm pull.

Hoop/wand raise over head, side and back, hoop/wand stretch and pass through, coordinator jumping jacks, gymnastic activities, i.e., balance beam, parallel bars.

Team sports involving raising arms, such as underhand volleyball serve.

3.532 Flex and extend the elbow.

3.532 Movement exploration, i.e., push yourself into a stand or squat, push from prone to supine position, push-ups, chin-ups, pull-ups, catching a ball. Frisbee toss, basketball chest pass, basketball one hand push shot, batting (softball), hockey drive, volleying (volleyball), gymnastic activities, i.e., vaulting and beam mounts.

112

3.533 Circumduct the arm at the
       shoulder in a full circle.

3.533 Movement exploration: i.e., how
       can you make your arm swing, how
       big a circle can your arm swing in.
       Use over exaggeration of arms
       using various locomotor skills,
       arm circles, hoop spin on arm, long
       rope turning, overhand throw with
       ball, softball throw (fitness test),
       overhead volleyball serve and spike.

3.534 Rotate the forearm.

3.534 Movement exploration: How do you
       turn your forearm and show differ-
       ent ways to move it. Forearm
       rotation push (rotate, push, pull),
       balloon bounce, paddle hit ball to
       self (turning palm up then down
       each time).

3.535 Flex, extend and rotate
       the wrist.

3.535 Movement exploration: How can you
       bend your wrist? Show different
       ways it can move. Scoop activities.
       Parachute: Ripples and Waves,
       Popcorn, Wind it Up.

       Rope turning, jumprope with hoop,
       paddle hit to wall and rebound,
       refer to 3.312 experiences and use
       bean bag and ball activities, hoop
       spin to self, dribbling a ball,
       lummi sticks and tinikling, stick
       activities, basketball overhead pass,
       dribbling in hockey.

BEHAVIORAL OBJECTIVES (Students will be able to):	LEARNING EXPERIENCES
3.536 Raise the leg(s) sideward/ upward, forward/upward and backward/upward.	3.536 Movement exploration: How many different ways can you raise and move your legs? Crab kicking, leg raisers (side flex), leg lifts, half lever on horizontal ladder, instep kick - soccer, outside foot kick (soccer), punt (football and soccer).
3.537 Flex, extend and rotate the knee.	3.537 Movement exploration: How many different ways can you move the knees? Knee hug, turk stand, loco-motor skills, rabbit hop, treadmills, scooter travel, mule kick, heel click, knee dip, ready positions, knee trap - soccer.
3.538 Flex, extend and rotate the ankle.	3.538 Movement exploration: Can you walk on toes, heels, etc.?

Locomotor skills, Beat Goes On, toe raisers, heel raisers, greet the toe, ready positions, soccer trap, La Raspa, grapevine step, pivot turn on beam, leap on beam. |

3.54 Extremities

3.541 Extend, flex and separate (abduction-adduction) the fingers.

Movement exploration: How can you move your fingers in different ways? Fist clenches, parachute (merry-go-round), grips, scooter push with hands, rope climbing, peg board.

3.542 Extend, flex and separate (abduction-adduction) the toes.

Movement exploration: How many different ways can you move your toes? Tiptoe walk, tire jump (bare-foot), (in/out), towel gripping, ping-pong ball passing, drawing forms on paper with toes.

3.60 Kinesthesis

3.61 Demonstrate awareness of position of body parts and body in performance of non-locomotor tasks, i.e., swinging, twisting, walking, running.

Movement exploration: How many ways can you move your arms and keep them moving until told to stop?

Parachute activities, tug-of-war, stunts and tumbling activities, wring-dish-rag.

Rhythms - do Hokie Pokie, Farmer in the Dell.

PHYSICAL DEVELOPMENT

BEHAVIORAL OBJECTIVES (Students will be able to):	LEARNING EXPERIENCES
	Low Organized games - Mickey Mouse, freeze tag.
	Apparatus - rope, parallel bars, horizontal ladder.
	Baseball, soccer, track and field activities.
3.62 Demonstrate awareness of position of body parts and body in the performance of object handling tasks.	3.62 Use experiences in 3.312 with emphasis on body and body parts in relation with objects.
3.63 Demonstrate awareness of position of body and body parts in differing environments (land, air, ice, water).	3.63 Movement exploration: How would you move in: mud or on ice, or in water, etc.?
	Leaping to explored poses evolving to specific responses.
	Sliding to explored poses evolving to specific responses.
	Trampoline activities; exploration of basic patterns evolving to specific skill development and sequencing of patterns.
	Dance in exploration to specific skills to creative sequenced movements.

3.70 Rhythm

3.71 Self-Imposed

116

3.711   Perform sustained and percussive movements at own tempo with non-locomotor and locomotor skills.

3.711   Problem solving such as: ask child to rise in a sustained manner (slowly) and repeat rising in a percussive manner (quickly); mimetics such as pushing, pulling, striking in "slow motion" and repeat above movements "sharply," running into a vertical jump.

3.712   Rhythmic consistency in repetition of pattern.

3.712   Problem solving to arrive at consistent pattern performance, i.e., running, skipping, striking. Combine another movement with identified rhythm movement (clap and skip). Evolve rhythm movement to goal direction performance (approach to vault, batting a ball).

3.72   Externally Imposed

3.721   Respond to specific time signatures with non-locomotor and locomotor patterns and skills.

3.721   Simple movements (as in 3.212) in response to clapping, drumming or recorded music which incorporates various beat patterns (2/4, 3/4, 4/4, 6/8), singing games, folk dance, free movement and creative dance.

3.722   Respond to above time signatures with object handling tasks.

3.722   Using above time signatures and sounds with locomotor movements listed in 3.221 including the following objects: ribbons, wands, poi-poi's, balls, lummi sticks, hoops, jump ropes, parachute.

3.723   Respond to changes in tempo using non-locomotor and loco-motor movements.

3.723   Using movements listed in 3.221 by varying fast, medium, slow tempos.

117

PHYSICAL DEVELOPMENT

BEHAVIORAL OBJECTIVES (Students will be able to):

LEARNING EXPERIENCES

3.724 Respond to changes in tempo maintaining a rhythm pattern using objects.

3.724 Using objects listed in 3.722 varying tempo (fast, medium, slow).

3.725 Incorporate response to time signatures and changes in tempo utilizing locomotor and non-locomotor patterns into specific dance steps or dances.

3.725 Use the following dance steps: polka, Schottishe, two step, step-hop, waltz, waltz balance in such dances as Kinder-polka, Dance of Greeting, Chimes of Dunkirk, Jessie Polka.

3.80 Strength

3.81 Sufficient arm strength to lift, push or pull one's own body weight.

3.81 Movement exploration: Can you support your body weight using only your hands and arms for support? Can you move across the floor using only your hands and arms? Etc.

Stunts: Alligator, seal crawl, crab walk, elbow crawl, coffee grinder, turtle, knee drop, dead man fall, wheelbarrow, bridge, L-seat, elbow balance, frog stand, hand stand, pyramids. Push ups, pull ups, chin ups, horizontal ladder, rope climbing, balance beam mounts, vaulting horse, horizontal bar-front arm support.

3.82 Sufficient leg strength to support one's own body weight for daily living tasks and survival requirements.

3.82 Movement exploration: Can you bounce up and down like a ball? Can you jump like a pogo stick, etc.?

118

Individual stunts: bouncing ball, pogo stick, frog jump, kangaroo jump, Russian dance, forward leg balance, single knee balance, etc.

Partner stunts: flying Dutchman, front sit, back layout, angel, distance running, rope jumping, inverted hangs, tinikling.

3.83   Movement exploration: How many different ways can you move across the room using your hands and feet at the same time?

Individual stunts: puppy dog run, lame dog walk, crab walk, spider walk, hand and knee balance.

Partner stunts: table, double bear, lighthouse, front sit, back layout. Pyramids, horizontal bar, parallel bars, vaulting, rope climbing.

3.91   Lifting: small objects—balls, bags, clubs, ropes, paper wads, etc. large objects – boxes, balls, mats, chair, etc.

Pushing: pushing a student on scooter board, pushing objects, (box, piano, etc.).

Pulling: Tug-of-War, pulling a student on scooter, pulling different objects across surface.

3.83   Sufficient total body strength to meet daily living tasks and survival requirements.

3.90   Power

3.91   Lift, push, pull, or swing varying weighted objects with required arm speed and force.

119

PHYSICAL DEVELOPMENT

BEHAVIORAL OBJECTIVES (Students will be able to):	LEARNING EXPERIENCES
	Swing: swinging a rope, bat, racquets, sticks, etc.
3.92 Propel or move the body by use of the arms with speed and force requirements.	3.92 Seal walk, elbow dip, push up, rope climbing, cargo net activities, parallel bars, physical educator, combatives, etc.
3.93 Perform leg movements to propel or move the body.	3.93 Jump the brook, jump over a rope, jump a stick, vertical jumps, heel clicks, frog jump, sprints, combatives, jumping (long jump, high jump, hurdles, etc.) vaulting, etc.
3.94 Perform leg movements to propel or move different objects.	3.94 Kicking, pushing, swinging at balls.
3.95 Perform efficiently tasks requiring coordinated body power (arms, legs and total body).	3.95 Same as 3.90 - 3.94.

4.0 BODY HANDLING DEVELOPMENT

4.10 Sensori-Motor Abilities

4.11 Body Awareness

4.111 Purposeful arm movements separately simultaneously and in alternation.	4.111 Arms Separately: mirroring, stretching, reaching, circles, axial movements with arms, arm wrestling, mimetics, hammering, pushing, pulling, punching, animals.

Arms Alternating: axial movements mirroring, stretching, reaching, circles; mimetics: swimming crawl stroke, wheelbarrow, punching; horizontal ladder walk, parallel bars walk, blocking in basketball defense.

Arms Simultaneously: axial movements, stretching, reaching, circles, mimetics: birds, airplane, arm assistance in jumping and hopping, pull-ups, chin-ups, arm dips, breat stroke.

4.112 Perform purposeful leg movements separately, simultaneously and in alternation.

4.112 Legs Separately: mirroring: leg lifts, twists, stretching, bending, mid-point crossing, other axial movements, high kicks, leg lifts, lying on side, bend left, bend and straighten, leg lifts; mimetics: kicking, swinging, balance stands, stork, airplane, foot to knee; hop for distance, one leg squat on floor or apparatus, single leg jump through, leg wrestling.

Legs Simultaneously: Pretzel bend, hip roll, V-seat, legs pulled to chest, mimetics: mule kick, swimming frog kick.

Legs Alternation: mimetics: leg flutters, bicycling, skating, scissors; locomotor movement, exploration without use of arms.

4.113 Perform purposeful arm and leg movements together, unilaterally, bilaterally and cross-laterally.

4.113 Unilaterally: bear walk, crab walk, crawling, exploring other locomotor movements with one side of body. mimetics: basketball shooting,

121

BODY HANDLING DEVELOPMENT

BEHAVIORAL OBJECTIVES (Student will be able to):	LEARNING EXPERIENCES
	pushing, pulling; games, standing Indian wrestling, hop tag; creative dance using different movements (vibratory movements, single and combination, etc.).
	Bilaterally: dog walk, crawling, alligator, seal, frog, kangaroo, angels-in-the-snow, dance swings, vertical jump, 1/4-1/2-3/4 and full top spins, take-off and landings; standing long jump, running long jump, high jump, diving rolls, straddle vault, leap frog, relays, volleyball blocking; tumbling and gymnastics; rolls, cartwheels, walkovers, walking on hands, hand springs, wolf mount on beam, hip circles, running and positioning in sports (hockey, soccer, etc.).
	Crosslateral: locomotor patterns using exploration, dodging, feinting, cheerleader (chorus girl) routines, Charleston or other dance patterns.
4.114 Perform purposeful movements with body segments separately and together.	4.114 Warm-up exercises: shoulder lifts, angle stretches, jumping jacks, heel-toe step in place, knee to elbow touch; in a game with a partner; back to back; problem solving with group (making shapes, etc.).

4.115   Perform a locomotor pattern while moving the trunk or arms in a non-locomotor pattern.

Mimetics and mirroring: walk and swing arms, run and punch, jump and circle arms, seat walk and trunk twist, Cut-the Cake, Beater Goes Round, Squirrels in Trees, Tag Games; dash or springs.

4.12   Body in Relation to Space

4.121   Change body size and shape to a given space.

Geometric shapes; with hoops, tires, boxes, ropes; make designs on floor and make self look like; fill in the space made by the shape; make self tall, short, fat, etc.; positional play in sports (football, soccer, etc.) and dance.

4.122   Select movements appropriate to varying sizes and shapes of space.

Discrimination course: run or walk on large and small carpet tiles; obstacle course; games: freeze, in and out the window, stepping stones, skin the snake, walking on a rope.

4.123   Demonstrate the appropriate facing level and locomotor pattern through a variety of spaces without over-estimating or under-estimating own size.

Obstacle courses exploring varying space types such as going through a large refrigerator carton, bicycle tire, hoops, double door, ladder rungs, between chairs, through spaces on climbing apparatus; children set up own obstacle course; Limbo.

4.13   Body in Relation to Surrounding Objects

4.131   Perform the movement of body parts in a variety of space sizes without touching anyone or anything.

Teacher directed axial movements and movements of body parts in large space; with partner in small space; problem solving; creative movements involving movements of body parts in specific space sizes.

123

BODY HANDLING DEVELOPMENT

BEHAVIORAL OBJECTIVES (Student will be able to):

LEARNING EXPERIENCES

4.132 Perform locomotor patterns and skills among people without bumping or losing balance in changing spaces.

4.132 Games: freeze, windows, squirrels, germ and toothbrush, streets and alleys; sports activities: discriminate positions.

4.133 Move through, over or around a maze or obstacle course without losing control.

4.133 Scooter riding in varying positions over carpets and ropes, under benches. Run through maze of cones, traverse the jungle gym, select varying objects to use as stepping stones over specified distance. Have students make maze or obstacle course with own bodies and have and have one student traverse the maze, alternate.

4.134 Dodge/evade another person or object.

4.134 Play tag, dodgeball, use feinting and dodging tactics in sports activities.

4.14 Discrimination

4.141 Auditory

4.1411 Move body/body parts in response to beat of metronome, drum, hand claps or other percussive instrument.

4.1411 Move head, shoulders, arms separately or in combinations to the steady beat in varying time signatures; above to underlying beat; move one body part to steady beat and one to the underlying beat; work in small group and have each member respond to a specific beat and/or part of group responding to specific steady beat and part to specific underlying beat.

4.1412	Move body/body parts in response to change of tempo.	4.1412	Use activities listed in 1.1411 with changing speed: fast to slow, slow to medium, various combinations.
4.1413	Move body/body parts in response to changes in tone or intensity.	4.1413	Using locomotor patterns creatively mimic sounds of drum beats or of various records such as: Elephant Walk, Pink Panther, Popcorn, Flight of the Bumblebee.
4.1414	Perform movements with appropriate force to pre-assigned differing sounds.	4.1414	Using triangles, drums, sticks, shakers, castanets, bells, do assigned locomotor and non-locomotor tasks, as stamp on drum beat, shake on triangle sounds, etc.
4.1415	Perform movements in appropriate direction to pre-assigned differing sounds.	4.1415	Using records or instruments as in 1.1414 vary movements of pre-determined directions, e.g., move forward to triangle, backward to bells, sideward to drums, in circle to castanets.
4.1416	Perform movements at appropriate level to pre-assigned different sounds.	4.1416	Using records or instruments as in 4.1414 vary movements with changing levels, e.g., move on tiptoes to bells, crawl to drum, etc.
4.1417	Perform movements at appropriate speed to pre-assigned differing sounds.	4.1417	Using records or instruments as in 4.1414 vary movements with changing speeds, e.g., move quickly to triangles, slowly to drums, etc.

4.142 Visual

4.1421	Follow a moving object or person.	4.1421	Play follow the leader, follow the flight of an arrow, a ball, balloon, etc.

BODY HANDLING DEVELOPMENT

BEHAVIORAL OBJECTIVES (Student will be able to):	LEARNING EXPERIENCES
4.1422 Visually follow a moving object or person and make contact with it with a body part.	4.1422 Tag games, play tether ball, play kicking games, hitting games, modified sports, e.g., soccer, basketball, etc.
4.143 Tactile Differentiate among varying surfaces and objects by varying locomotor skills and speeds by making adjustments in handling objects.	4.143 Change surfaces (gravel, sand, grass, gym floor) for individual student to use locomotor skills (walk, run, slide, etc.). Same as above with partner; with a group. Problem solving on different surfaces using different locomotor skills at different speeds. Problem solving, i.e., can a student hold a ping pong ball with one hand, five inch wiffle ball with one hand, squeeze yarn ball with one hand and hold, hold same ball with both hands.
4.144 Kinesthetic	
4.1441 Perform non-locomotor and locomotor tasks with awareness of the body/body part positioning.	4.1441 Imitation of movement/mirroring of movements of body parts, modified "Simon says", move body or body parts on command without looking. Problem solving of preparatory, execution and follow through movement for specific activity skills (sports, dance, gymnastics, track, etc.).
4.1442 Make adjustments in positioning of body/body parts as changes occur in speed, direction, force, level, in the	4.1442 Set tasks involving changes in speed, direction, force, level and have students working with partners check ability to make positioning changes.

126

performance of non-locomotor and locomotor tasks.

Use game skills, modified dances, track activities, etc. with varying requirements of limb positioning changes, changes in limb speed, body positioning, etc.

4.20 Non-Locomotor Patterns and Skills

4.21 Exhibit postural control in standing, sitting, kneeling, squatting, inverted standing and lying, through the stages of arriving at the specific position.

4.21 Have children experiment with different ways of standing, sitting, lying, etc., discuss efficiency and inefficiency of each; have children progress from lying to sit, sit to stand, stand to kneel, kneel to headstand and similar combinations while remaining in the same spot.

4.22 Exhibit postural control throughout the stages of pre-action, in-action and post-action in the performance of activities which require movements of the body segments and body parts in a non-locomotor situation.

4.22 Have children create or imitate movements such as winding up and unwinding a rubber band, being a tree in a windstorm. Have children perform simple stunts like a scale, corkscrew; perform leg splits while in a headstand position.

See 1.21, 1.225, 3.611 and bring attention to timing of trunk/hip rotation in batting, joint flexion in catching, body torque for creative dance movements, etc.

4.30 Locomotor Patterns and Skills

4.31 Perform the basic locomotor patterns and pattern variations in an efficient manner for a variety of task requirements (e.g., change of direction, change of level, variation in speed).

4.31 Individual problem solving; response to teacher command; rhythm games and games involving changes of speed and/or direction, level. Shuttle races.

See experiences listed for 1.22, 3.10, 3.22, 3.33.

BODY HANDLING DEVELOPMENT

BEHAVIORAL OBJECTIVES (Student will be able to):	LEARNING EXPERIENCES
4.32 Combine locomotor patterns in an efficient and controlled manner for effective propulsion (increase of power, speed, distance); e.g., run and jump; hop-step-jump; etc.	4.32 Creative movement problems combining patterns (with or without rhythmic accompaniment); track events; tasks on gymnastic apparatus; skill practice and/or participation in team and individual games requiring these abilities. See experiences for 1.211, 1.311, 1.321.
4.33 Combine locomotor patterns in an efficient and controlled manner for effective absorption (reduction of speed, power, distance) e.g., run and stop, leap and fall, skip and slide, etc.	4.33 Run and jump onto crash pad; problem solving combining run or skip with a controlled slide. Activities for vaulting or gymnastic apparatus, activities on mini-tramp. Set up individual and dual games, creative movement routines and dances requiring force absorption. See experiences for 1.221, 1.231.
4.40 Combining Locomotor and Nonlocomotor Patterns and Skills	
4.41 Perform a locomotor pattern while performing a non-locomotor pattern with the arms (swinging, slashing, jabbing, pushing, etc.).	4.41 Movement Exploration: show different ways to move arms while performing locomotor movements, i.e., march using swinging, slashing, jabbing, pulling and pushing with arms; move like a bird; jumpnastics; rope jumping, parachute activities, mushroom, LaRaspa; Paw Paw Patch, Hokey Pokey, Bear Song, Virginia Reel; basketball

dribble, basketball guarding; **volleyball** spike, high jump, floor exercise.

4.42 Perform a locomotor pattern or skill while performing a non-locomotor pattern or skill with body segments as in trunk bending/stretching, trunk rotation, head nodding, head swinging, hip swaying, etc.

4.42 Movement Exploration: show different ways to move body segments while performing locomotor skills, i.e., walking high and low, move like a clown, elephant, frog.

Rolling, and bowling, parachute (Inside the Mountain), Squirrels in Trees, dodgeball, leap frog, creative "rhythms:" listening and reacting to various types of music, i.e., computer music and mood music.

London Bridge, Seven Jumps, Hora.

Gymnastics: tumbling, balance beam, floor exercise.

Hockey, basketball, volleyball bump and dig, shot put, high jump.

4.50 Combining Locomotor/Non-Locomotor/Body Awareness

4.51 Laterality

4.511 Perform unilateral use of arms and legs (side vs. side, and upper vs. lower or total body) while performing a locomotor and non-locomotor activity.

4.511 Movement Exploration: can you move one side of the body at a time using locomotor and non-locomotor skills, i.e., robot walk, bear walk. Using the same movements can you move upper and lower parts of the body at the same time or different times, i.e., jumping jacks, mule kick, inch worm.

Mickey Mouse, relays; creative rhythms, stilt walking, forward

BODY HANDLING DEVELOPMENT

BEHAVIORAL OBJECTIVES   (Student will be able to):   LEARNING EXPERIENCES

roll, cartwheel, handstand, handspring, hip circles (front and back),
skin the cat on the bars.

4.512 Perform activities which involve bilateral use of arms
while performing locomotor and
non-locomotor activities to
increase distance, speed, or
assist in lift of the body.

4.512 Movement Exploration: show different
ways to move the body to increase
distance, speed or to lift the body,
i.e., can you hop from one point to
another? Can you hop there faster?
How high can you hop? Can you do
jumping turns?

Jump and hop relays; jump the brook;
obstacle course: hoops, tires and
ropes; jumping boards, mini-tramp,
creative rhythms, standing long jump,
vaulting, volleyball block.

4.513 Perform cross-lateral use of arms
and legs, as in one foot takeoff
in horizontal jumps, leaps.

4.513 Movement Exploration: show different
ways to move arms and legs in opposition, i.e., walk, run, skip, leap,
one-foot takeoff.

Relays, Charlie Over the Water,
Mickey Mouse; Farmer in the Dell,
Grand March, Grand Right and Left;
activities on horizontal ladder,
cargo net; floor exercise; walk, run,
leap on walking beam or olympic beam,
sports: hurdles, basketball, volleyball, softball.

4.52 Balance

130

4.521 Maintain balance and continuity in locomotor movement combined with bilateral non-locomotor movements.

Movement Exploration: while performing a locomotor movement with non-locomotor bilateral arm movements, maintain balance and continuity. Refer to 3.221 experiences using bilateral arm movements and to 4.512. In addition, may use: jumping turns on tire; hopping turns in and out of tire; rope jumping routines; mini-tramp skills; skills on balance beam.

4.522 Maintain balance and continuity in tasks which require cross-lateral arm/leg movements.

Refer to 3.221, 3.222, 3.223 and 4.513 stressing balance and continuity.

4.60 Movement Communication

4.61 Imitation of others' movements as a way of communication and as a process of learning.

Movement Exploration: can you portray an animal, person or thing?

Story mimetics: Raggedy Ann and Andy, Fire! Fire! Lemonade-Show Your Trade, Charades.

Poetic interpretations; musical interpretations; floor exercise, modern dance.

4.62 Utilization of expressive movement skills and combinations of movement skills to reflect or create self or expression of others.

Problem Solving: can you be happy, sad, etc. and express it with your face...with body parts...with total body?

Can you move using non-locomotor and locomotor skills to express emotions, feelings?

Reflect emotions, moods portrayed by visual stimuli (colors, pictures) and auditory stimuli (recordings, screams, piano tunes). Modern dance; exercise.

BODY HANDLING DEVELOPMENT

BEHAVIORAL OBJECTIVES (Student will be able to):		LEARNING EXPERIENCES	
4.63	Utilization of imitative and expressive movement skills and combinations of movement skills to enhance movement form or expression and increase movement function.	4.63	Refer to **4.61** and **4.62** experiences. Can also use the following: pantomime, mimes and non-lateral dance form of modern dance.

5.0 OBJECT HANDLING DEVELOPMENT

5.10	Demonstrate sensori-motor abilities.	5.10	See 4.10.
5.11	Perceive Visually		
5.111	Perceive oncoming objects in forward and peripheral locations at ever increasing distances.	5.111	Refer to **3.311, 3.312, 3.322, 4.142** and emphasize object handling.
5.112	Adjust to readiness position for receipt of object with decreasing effort for visual stimuli.	5.112	Refer to **1.214, 1.224, 1.225, 3.311, 3.312** and **4.142** and **3.22** with emphasis on ready position of hands, arms, feet or legs - whichever will be receiving objects.
5.12	Perceive auditorially		
5.121	Attend to appropriate sounds which facilitate performance.	5.121	Use of jump ropes, balls, sticks, feet tempo of music and listening for sounds and changes in sounds which would indicate object handling movement. Non-movement (ball bouncing to clapping sound pattern;

132

ball bouncing movement to given music, jump ropes to given music) tinikling, folk dancing, basketball, softball.

5.122   Refer to 5.121 learning experiences and emphasize readiness position.

5.122   Respond to specific sounds by assuming readiness position with ever decreasing effort.

5.13   Have students learn the feeling of different objects in reference to shapes, texture, size and weight and experience those objects with receipt and propulsion activities (nerf ball, football, volleyball, etc...). Use those in: Animal chase, hot potato, captain ball.

5.13   Attend to tactile cues to increase motor judgment, decrease reaction time and increase generalizations.

5.14   Refer to 3.62, 5.11, 3.72 and 5.13. This would apply to mainly intermediate students and would be tested through skill tests covering object handling activities watching for kinesthetic awareness.

5.14   Indicate through appropriate responses kinesthetic perception through developed kinesthetic cueing.

5.20   Indicate Coordination

5.21   Refer to 3.312 learning experiences. Emphase preparation of hands before catching, use of hands while catching and use of hands once object is caught.

5.21   Demonstrate eye-hand perception indicated by preparation positioning - action-movement proficiency and after-movement control.

5.22   Refer to 3.322 learning experiences. Emphasize preparation of feet or foot before contact, during contact and after contact.

5.22   Demonstrate eye-foot perception indicated by preparation positioning, action-movement proficiency and after-movement control.

OBJECT HANDLING DEVELOPMENT

BEHAVIORAL OBJECTIVES (Student will be able to):		LEARNING EXPERIENCES	
5.30	Demonstrate Propulsion Ability		
5.31	Demonstrate accuracy in propelling an object through use of eye-hand and/or eye-foot skill incorporating force and timing.	5.31	Refer to 3.313, 3.314, 3.315, 3.316, 3.321, 3.322, 3.62 and use experiences emphasizing accuracy.
5.32	Demonstrate the ability to propel an object for distance through use of eye-hand and/or eye-foot skills incorporating force and timing.	5.32	Refer to 5.31 experiences and emphasize distance.
5.33	Demonstrate speed in repelling objects through use of eye-hand and/or eye-foot skills incorporating force and timing.	5.33	Refer to 5.31 experiences and emphasize speed.
5.40	Demonstrate Absorption of Force Ability		
5.41	Demonstrate control in absorbing force of oncoming objects with the hands in different and varying situations (speed and distance).	5.41	Refer to 3.312, 3.62. Emphasize control.
5.42	Demonstrate ability to control an oncoming object with an implement in the hand in more demanding situations of speed and distance.	5.42	Refer to 3.312.

6.0 COORDINATED BODY AND OBJECT HANDLING

6.10 Demonstrate Coordination

6.11 Receive, interpret and respond
using the hands correctly and
efficiently to various visual
stimuli.

6.11 Refer to 3.311 and 3.312 and perform
while in locomotion. Passing and
receiving lummi stick, rhythm games,
passing and receiving in relay.

Bounce and catch, toss and catch and
dribbling while using locomotor
skills by oneself.

Do all of the above with a partner.

Do all of the above in small groups
such as low organized games, hot
potato, circle call ball, sink the
ship, keep away, spud, catch the
cane, conquest, tetherball, or
drills and relays, box and ball,
obstacle course dribble, ball and
puck dribble, 3 or 5 man weave.

Do all of the previously listed
activities in teams.

Softball, hot box, Indian ball, three
grounders and a fly, beat ball, one
fly, one base (throwing) Danish
rounder.

Basketball, basketball relay, "21",
around the world, bombardment, pin
guard, hose.

Volleyball; Newcombe, volley tennis,
balloon, beach, cage balls, volleyball.

Football; hike and pass, football,
baseball, Line ball, aerial ball.

Hockey, scooter hockey, hoc-soc, end
zone hockey, hit and run, nobbies.

COORDINATED BODY AND OBJECT HANDLING

BEHAVIORAL OBJECTIVES   (Student will be
                          able to):

                          LEARNING EXPERIENCES

6.12 Receive, interpret and respond with   6.12 Refer to 3.321 and 3.322 while per-
      feet to visual stimuli.   forming locomotor skills. Jump, kick,
                                                     dribble, block, trap while using
                                                     locomotor skills with oneself. Do
                                                     all the above activities with
                                                     partners.

6.20 Demonstrate propulsion of object-
      locomotion

6.21 Accurately propel objects with   6.21 Do all the above in small groups,
      feet and/or hands.   such as low organized games, circle
                                                     stride ball, jump the shot, ball jump,
                                                     roll dodge ball, hopscotch, jump the
                                                     brook, magic carpets, weathervane.

                                                     Drills and relays. Do all listed in
                                                     6.11 using feet. Do all the above
                                                     in teams.

                                                     Soccer, speedball, line kick, line
                                                     soccer, long base, end ball, mass
                                                     soccer, crab soccer, scooter soccer,
                                                     kickball.

                                                     Football - punt across, kick over,
                                                     baseball, capture the foot-
                                                     ball, kick-off football, jump the
                                                     shot, ball and bean bag target toss,
                                                     tetherball games, ring toss, run the
                                                     gauntlet.

                                                     Team sport activities. Basketball,
                                                     lay ups, fast break, passing for
                                                     accuracy, 3 and 5 man weave, 1 on 1.

Soccer - run and shooting for goal, passing for accuracy, punting for accuracy, throw-ins for accuracy, line soccer, zone soccer.

Volleyball - spiking, blocking, bump or dig, set, newcombe, "keep it up", volley tennis, etc.

Softball - throwing.

6.22   Propel an object over increasing distances with feet/hands while moving.

6.22   Individual toss, run and catch activities, using wall and varied distances throw and catch the rebound, kicking different objects for distance (deflated balls, tin cans, etc...) kicking some object to graduated distances.

Drills and relays - distance toss of bean bags, etc., over-under relay, changing distance between players, refer to 6.21 for additional activities.

Football - punt, pass and kick contest.

Softball - base throwing, infield - outfield throwing.

Track and field softball throw, basketball throw, javelin (bamboo poles), shot put, baton pass.

Soccer - corner kicks, fullback kicks, drop kick, punt, penalty kick, place kick, throw-in, goalie throw.

6.23   Increase the speed of objects when propelling them with hand/foot while moving.

6.23   Refer to 3.221 and the above 6.22 activities using various speeds to compare distances and accuracy.

COORDINATED BODY AND OBJECT HANDLING

BEHAVIORAL OBJECTIVES   (Student will be
                         able to):

LEARNING EXPERIENCES

6.30   Demonstrate object absorption—
       locomotion.

6.31   Control body weight and the
       force of oncoming object while
       throwing and/or receiving said
       object.

6.31   Refer to 6.22 and do activities
       while adjusting body momentum and
       making visual discriminations.

Chapter Nine

Hazelwood Charts

The contents of this chapter represents the final step for the Hazelwood curriculum committee. The charts are composed of taxonomic numbers assigned to children by days, weeks, grade levels, and sexes. All Hazelwood physical educators received these charts and the content of chapter eight, the Hazelwood behavioral objectives and learning experiences. The charts showed the categories and items that were to be considered in the planning of learning experiences for children. The behavioral objectives and learning experiences of chapter eight could be modified by each teacher to fit the children with whom they worked, but the items and categories were to be covered in planning for the children at each school. The content of the program, the acquisitions of the children, and the worth of a teacher could theoretically be measured by monitoring the application of the charts.

The reader is again reminded that this chapter is a composite of one district committee's efforts in curriculum design. It has good points and bad points, but most of all, it reflects the needs of the children in that district. The children everywhere in the world have commonalities but, the authors have not seen one child anywhere that looked like a bell curve. Curriculum development should be specific to the needs of particular children. These charts are presented only as a model for comparison to the curricula designed by the readers of this work.

CHART 1	1.0 MENTAL	2.0 SOCIAL-EMOTIONAL	3.0 PHYSICAL	4.0 BODY-HANDLING	5.0 OBJECT-HANDLING	6.0 COORDINATED BODY-OBJECT	NOTES:
WEEK 1-2 GRADE K	1.11,1.12,1.13, 1.15,1.18 1.211,1.212, 1.213,1.221, 1.222 1.41,1.47 1.511,1.512, 1.513,1.53 1.652	2.11, 2.131 2.21, 2.23 2.32	3.11, 3.12 3.21,3.221, 3.222 3.33 3.52, 3.53	4.11, 4.131, 4.132 4.20 4.31 4.61			No equipment used. 1.51-Use of playground equipment only! No equipment in class.
WEEK 1-2 GRADES 1-2	1.11,1.12,1.13, 1.15,1.18 1.211,1.212,1.213, 1.221,1.222 1.41,1.42,1.46, 1.47 1.511,1.512,1.513, 1.531,1.533 1.652	2.11 2.131 2.21, 2.23 2.32, 2.35	As above plus 3.42 3.51,3.52,3.53, 3.54	4.10 4.20 4.31 4.61			No equipment
WEEK 1-2 GRADE 3	1.13,1.14,1.15, 1.16,1.17,1.18 1.211,1.212,1.213, 1.221,1.222, 1.231 1.311,1.312,1.313 1.40,1.46 1.511,1.512,1.513, 1.53 1.652	2.11, 2.13 2.20 2.32, 2.33, 2.34, 2.35 2.50	3.10 3.21,3.221,3.222 3.33 3.40, 3.42 3.52, 3.53 3.80 3.93	4.11,4.12,4.131, 4.132,4.144 4.20 4.30 4.61			No equipment
WEEK 1 GRADE 4	1.213,1.221 1.41,1.42,1.43, 1.44,1.45,1.46, 1.47 1.511,1.512,1.513, 1.531,1.532, 1.533 1.661,1.662,1.663, 1.664,1.665	2.111,2.112, 2.121,2.122, 2.123,2.124, 2.131,2.132, 2.141 2.21,2.23,2.24 2.321,2.322, 2.331,2.332, 2.341,2.342, 2.351,2.352	3.10 3.20 3.30 3.40 3.50 3.60 3.80 3.90	4.11,4.12,4.13, 4.14 4.20 4.30 4.40 4.50 4.61	5.10 5.20 5.30 5.40	6.10 6.20 6.30	Stress Orientation and development of basic concepts/procedures. Incorporate 3.0, 4.0,5.0 to enhance 1.0 and 2.0
WEEK 1 GRADE 5-6	As for GRADE 4	As for GRADE 4	As for GRADE 4	As for GRADE 4	As for GRADE 4	As for GRADE 4	As for GRADE 4

CHART 2

	1.0 MENTAL	2.0 SOCIAL-EMOTIONAL	3.0 PHYSICAL	4.0 BODY-HANDLING	5.0 OBJECT-HANDLING	6.0 COORDINATED BODY-OBJECT	NOTES:
WEEKS 3-7 GRADE K	1.14,1.16,1.17, 1.18 1.211,1.212,1.213, 1.214, 1.22, 1.231 1.42,1.44 1.512,1.513,1.514, 1.52,1.53 1.611,1.612,1.631, 1.634,1.661, 1.662,1.663	2.122,2.132 2.22,2.23,2.24,2.35 2.33,2.34,2.35 2.40 2.50	3.13,3.14 3.223 3.31 3.541 3.60 3.91	4.12,4.134,4.142, 4.143 4.50,4.52	5.13 5.21 5.30 5.40	6.11	5.30(eye-hand only, not eye-foot)
WEEKS 3-7 GRADES 1-2	1.14,1.16,1.17, 1.18 1.211,1.212,1.213, 1.214, 1.22, 1.231 1.31,1.32,1.33, 1.34 1.512,1.513,1.514, 1.52,1.53 1.611,1.612,1.613, 1.631,1.634, 1.661,1.662, 1.663	2.122,2.123, 2.132 2.22,2.23,2.24 2.33,2.34 2.40 2.50	As Above	4.12,4.134,4.142, 4.143,4.144 4.50,4.52	5.111,5.112,5.13 5.21 5.30 5.40	6.11	As Above
WEEKS 3-7 GRADE 3	1.14,1.16,1.17, 1.18 1.211,1.212,1.213, 1.214,1.22,1.23 1.31,1.32,1.33, 1.34 1.512,1.513,1.514, 1.52,1.53 1.613,1.631,1.634, 1.661,1.662, 1.663	2.121,2.122,2.123 2.23,2.24 2.311 2.40	3.223 3.31 3.541 3.60 3.91	4.134,4.142,4.143 4.40 4.50,4.52	As for GRADES 1-2	6.11 6.30	As above

	1	2	3	4	5	6	Notes
WEEKS 2-3 **GRADE 4**	1.17,1.18 1.21,1.211,1.212, 1.213,1.221, 1.222,1.225, 1.233 1.311,1.313,1.321 1.41,1.42,1.43, 1.44,1.45,1.46, 1.47 1.511,1.512,1.513, 1.53 1.66	2.10 2.20 2.311,2.312,2.32	3.10 3.20 3.30 3.40 3.50 3.60 3.70 3.80 3.90	4.111,4.112,4.113, 4.114,4.115, 4.1441,4.1442 4.21,4.22 4.31,4.32,4.33 4.41,4.42 4.511,4.512,4.513	5.12,5.121 5.20 5.30 5.40	6.10 6.20 6.30	When broad areas are listed (ex. 2.10) all sub areas should be generally reviewed. However, if some sub areas need continued attention (i.e.,2.11)
WEEKS 2-3 **GRADES 5-6**	1.17,1.18 1.21,1.211,1.212, 1.213,1.221, 1.222,1.225, 1.231,1.233 1.311,1.313,1.321 1.41,1.42,1.43, 1.44,1.45,1.46, 1.47 1.511,1.512,1.513, 1.53 1.66	2.10 2.20 2.311,2.312,2.313, 2.314,2.321, 2.322,2.34, 2.35 2.40 2.50	As for GRADE 4	As for GRADE 4 plus: 4.521,4.522	As for GRADE 4	6.10 6.20 6.30	Such attention should be given along with general Review of other sub-areas.

CHART 3	1.0 MENTAL	2.0 SOCIAL-EMOTIONAL	3.0 PHYSICAL	4.0 BODY-HANDLING	5.0 OBJECT-HANDLING	6.0 COORDINATED BODY-OBJECT	NOTES:
WEEKS 8-12 GRADE K	1.33,1.34 1.41,1.43,1.47 1.514,1.52,1.53 1.631,1.633,1.634, 1.66	2.11,2.123,2.14 2.40	3.12 3.32,3.33 3.536,3.537,3.538, 3.542 3.60 3.93,3.94	4.112,4.113,4.13, 4.142,4.144	5.111,5.112 5.22 5.30	6.12 6.20 6.30	Follow through with objectives from past seven weeks, but stress new and repeated objectives. During this period, stress eye-foot.
WEEKS 8-12 GRADES 1-2	As above	As above	As above	As above	As above	As above	
WEEKS 8-12 GRADE 3	As above	As above	As above	As above	As above	As above	As above
WEEKS 4-14 GRADE 4	1.16,1.17,1.18 1.211,1.212,1.214, 1.221,1.223, 1.224,1.225, 1.226,1.231, 1.232,1.233 1.311,1.312,1.313, 1.321,1.331, 1.341 1.40 1.511,1.512,1.513, 1.514,1.521, 1.522,1.523, 1.524,1.53, 1.66	2.10 2.20 2.311,2.312,2.313 2.314,2.321, 2.322,2.311, 2.322,2.34,2.35 2.41,2.42 2.50	3.11,3.12,3.13 3.221,3.222, 3.223,3.311, 3.312,3.313, 3.314,3.315 3.316,3.321, 3.322,3.331, 3.332 3.40 3.50 3.611,3.62,3.63 3.712 3.80 and 3.90	4.11,4.112,4.113, 4.121,4.132, 4.134,4.1421, 4.1422,4.1423, 4.143,4.144 4.31,4.32,4.33 4.41,4.42 4.512,4.513	5.111,5.112,5.12, 5.13,5.14 5.21,5.22 5.31,5.32,5.33 5.41,5.42	6.11,6.12 6.21,6.22,6.23 6.31	
WEEKS 4-14 GRADES 5-6	As for GRADE 4	2.311,2.312,2.313, 2.314,2.321, 2.322,2.331, 2.332,2.34,2.35 2.41,2.42 2.50	As above for GRADE 4	As for GRADE 4	As for GRADE 4	As for GRADE 4	

CHART 4

CHART 4	1.0 MENTAL	2.0 SOCIAL-EMOTIONAL	3.0 PHYSICAL	4.0 BODY-HANDLING	5.0 OBJECT-HANDLING	6.0 COORDINATED BODY-OBJECT	NOTES:
WEEKS 18-29 GRADE K	1.14,1.16,1.17, 1.18 1.211,1.212,1.213, 1.215,1.216, 1.221,1.222, 1.225,1.231 1.31,1.32 1.42,1.44,1.45, 1.46,1.47 1.50 1.61,1.621,1.622, 1.623 1.631,1.634,1.64, 1.653	2.10 2.20 2.32,2.33 2.40	3.10 3.211,3.2120, 3.2130,3.2132, 3.2140,3.215, 3.221,3.222, 3.223,3.224 3.40 3.51,3.52,3.53, 3.54 3.60 3.70 3.80 and 3.90	4.11,4.12,4.141, 4.144 4.20 4.31 4.40 4.511,4.512,4.513, 4.521 4.60	5.12		Objectives may be the same for each grade level but learning experiences will vary.
WEEKS 13-29 GRADES 1-2	As above	As above	3.10 3.211,3.2120, 3.2121,3.2130, 3.2131,3.2132, 3.2140,3.2141, 3.215,3.221, 3.222,3.223, 3.224 3.40 3.51,3.52,3.53, 3.54 3.60 3.70 3.80 and 3.90	As above	5.12		Objectives in object handling have been covered in first twelve weeks. Emphasis is now on handling to rhythm.
WEEKS 13-19 GRADE 3	As above in categories 1.1, 1.2,1.3,1.4,1.5. As follows for 1.6: 1.623,1.631,1.632, 1.634,1.64, 1.653	2.10 2.20 2.311,2.312, 2.313,2.32, 2.33 2.40	3.10 3.2130,3.2131, 3.2141,3.215, 3.221,3.222, 3.223 3.40 3.51,3.52,3.53, 3.54 3.60 3.70 3.80 3.90	4.11,4.12,4.141, 4.144 4.20 4.32,4.33 4.40 4.50 4.60	5.12		

WEEKS 15-22 GRADE 4					
1.10 1.216,1.221,1.222 1.225,1.233 1.311,1.312, 1.313,1.321 1.40 1.50 1.61,1.66	2.11,2.12,2.13, 2.14,2.15 2.20 2.30 2.40 2.50	3.13,3.14 3.2110,3.2120, 3.212,3.2130, 3.2131,3.2132, 3.2140,3.2141, 3.2142,3.215, 3.216,3.22, 3.221,3.222, 3.223,3.224, 3.225 3.30 3.40,3.421,3.422 3.51,3.512,3.513 3.521,3.522,	4.111,4.112,4.113, 4.114,4.115, 4.13,4.1441, 4.1442 4.21,4.22 4.42 4.511,4.512,4.513, 4.521,4.522	5.10 5.20 5.30	6.10
WEEKS 15-22 GRADES 5-6					
As for GRADE 4	As for GRADE 4	3.523,3.531, 3.532,3.536, 3.537,3.538, 3.541 3.611,3.63 3.712 3.81,3.82,3.83, 3.91,3.92,3.93, 3.95	As above for GRADE 4	5.10 5.20 5.30	6.10

CHART 5	1.0 MENTAL	2.0 SOCIAL-EMOTIONAL	3.0 PHYSICAL	4.0 BODY-HANDLING	5.0 OBJECT-HANDLING	6.0 COORDINATED BODY-OBJECT	NOTES:
WEEKS 30-38 GRADE K	1.211,1.212,1.213, 1.22,1.23 1.50	2.124,2.13,2.14 2.32,2.34,2.35 2.50	3.11,3.312,3.313, 3.315,3.321, 3.33 3.40 3.611,3.612	4.132,4.133,4.134, 4.142 4.40 4.513	5.10,5.12,5.13 5.41	6.10	Follow through with objective from entire year that can be reemphasized but stress new and repeated objectives.
WEEKS 30-38 GRADE 1-2	As above	2.124,2.13,2.14 2.21,2.23 2.32,2.34,2.35 2.50	3.11,3.12,3.13 3.312,3.313, 3.314,3.315, 3.321,3.322, 3.33 3.40 3.611,3.612	As above plus 4.30	As above plus 5.20	6.10 6.20	#3.314 in 2nd grade only. Same as above
WEEKS 30-38 GRADE 3	1.25 1.30 1.50 1.633	2.124,2.13,2.14 2.21,2.23 2.31,2.32,2.33, 2.34,2.35 2.50	3.11,3.12,3.13, 3.312, 3.313, 3.314,3.315, 3.316,3.322, 3.33 3.40 3.611,3.612	4.132,4.133,4.134, 4.142,4.144 4.30 4.40 4.513	5.10,5.12,5.13 5.20 5.30 5.42	6.10 6.20 6.30	As above
WEEKS 23-28 GRADES 4-5 RHYTHMS	1.18 1.211,1.213,1.215, 1.222 1.511,1.522,1.523, 1.524 1.613,1.614,1.622, 1.64,1.66	2.12,2.14,2.15 2.20 2.30 2.40 2.50	3.11 3.538 3.711,3.712,3.721 3.722,3.723, 3.724,3.725	4.113,4.121,4.1411 4.1412,4.1413, 4.1414,4.1415, 4.1416,4.1417 4.22 4.30 4.41,4.42 4.50	5.121	6.31	Weeks 23-28 for 4th & 5th grade Rhythms
WEEKS 23-26 GRADE 6 RHYTHMS	As above	As above	3.216 3.538 3.711,3.712,3.721 3.722,3.723, 3.724,3.725	As above	5.121	6.31	Weeks 23-26 for 6th grade Rhythms

149

CHART 6	1.0 MENTAL	2.0 SOCIAL-EMOTIONAL	3.0 PHYSICAL	4.0 BODY-HANDLING	5.0 OBJECT-HANDLING	6.0 COORDINATED BODY-OBJECT	NOTES:
WEEKS 27-28 D A N C E	1.21,1.212,1.215, 1.222,1.312, 1.313,1.522, 1.523,1.613,1.614, 1.622,1.64, 1.66	2.123,2.124,2.134, 2.141,2.15,2.20, 2.312,2.32,2.33, 2.40,2.50	3.12,3.13,3.14, 3.20,3.30,3.40, 3.51,3.52,3.53, 3.54,3.60,3.711, 3.712,3.721, 3.722,3.723, 3.724,3.725	4.10 4.22,4.33,4.42, 4.511,4.512, 4.513,4.52 4.61,4.62,4.63	5.12		Modern Dance
GRADE 6 W R E S T L I N G	1.10,1.214,1.311, 1.312,1.313, 1.321,1.41,1.42, 1.43,1.44,1.45, 1.46,1.47,1.511, 1.512,1.513, 1.514,1.521,1.522, 1.523,1.531,1.532, 1.533,1.654,1.655, 1.66	2.10 2.20 2.30 2.40 2.50	3.10,3.20,3.31, 3.331,3.332, 3.411,3.412, 3.421,3.511, 3.522,3.523, 3.531,3.532, 3.533,3.534, 3.535,3.536, 3.537,3.538, 3.611,3.81,3.91, 3.92,3.93,3.95	4.111,4.112,4.113, 4.114,4.115,4.121, 4.134,4.1421, 4.1422,4.1442 4.41			Wrestling
WEEKS 29-34 GRADE 4	1.16,1.17,1.211, 1.212,1.214, 1.221,1.223, 1.224,1.225, 1.226,1.231, 1.232,1.233, 1.311,1.312, 1.313,1.321, 1.331,1.341, 1.40, 1.50, 1.634,1.66	2.131 2.20 2.311,2.312, 2.313,2.314,2.32, 2.352 2.41,2.42 2.50	3.12,3.13,3.20, 3.311,3.312, 3.313,3.314, 3.316,3.33, 3.411,3.412, 3.421,3.422,3.50, 3.60,3.70,3.80, 3.91,3.93,3.94, 3.95	4.111,4.113, 4.122,4.123, 4.132,4.142, 4.143,4.144, 4.32,4.41,4.42 4.513,4.52	5.111,5.112, 5.122 5.20 5.30 5.40	6.10 6.20,6.22 6.31	
WEEKS 29-34 GRADES 5-6	As above for GRADE 4	As for GRADE 4	As for GRADE 4	As for GRADE 4	As for GRADE 4	As for GRADE 4	

WEEKS 35–38 GRADE 4	1.231,1.232,1.233 1.311,1.312, 1.313,1.321,1.331, 1.341,1.40,1.511, 1.512,1.513,1.514, 1.521,1.522,1.523, 1.524,1.531,1.532, 1.533,1.63,1.65, 1.66	2.10 2.20 2.30 2.40 2.50	3.11,3.12,3.221, 3.222,3.223, 3.311,3.312, 3.313,3.314, 3.315,3.316, 3.331,3.332,3.40, 3.50,3.60 3.80,3.90	4.111,4.112, 4.113,4.114, 4.115,4.132, 4.134,4.1421, 4.1422,4.1423, 4.143,4.1441, 4.1442,4.22,4.31, 4.32,4.33,4.41, 4.42,4.513,4.52, 4.60	5.111,5.112, 5.121,5.122,5.13, 5.14,5.21,5.22, 5.31,5.32,5.33, 5.41,5.42	6.11,6.12 6.21,6.22,6.23 6.31
WEEKS 35–38 GRADES 5–6	As for GRADE 4	As for GRADE 4	As for GRADE 4	As for GRADE 4	As for GRADE 4	As for GRADE 4

Bibliography

American Alliance for Health, Physical Education and Recreation. Professional Preparation in Dance, Physical Education, Safety Education and School Health Education. (Report of 1973 Conference) Washington, D. C.: AAHPER, 1974.

Associated Organizations for Teacher Education. National Invitational Conference Preliminary Report: Redesigning Teacher Education. St. Louis, Missouri: AOTE, 1973.

Arnett, C. and M. M. Thompson. Perceptual Motor and Motor Performance Test Batteries Developed for Pre-School Through Grade Six Children. U. S. Department of Health, Education and Welfare, Office of Education, Bureau of Research, Project #8-F-008, Grant #OEG 6-9-008068, February, 1970.

Bloom, B. S. (Ed.) Taxonomy of Educational Objectives Handbook I: Cognitive Domain. New York: David McKay Company, Inc., 1956.

Bruner, J. S. "The Course of Cognitive Growth." American Psychologist. 19:1-15. January, 1964.

Center for the Study of Evaluation. Instructional Objectives Exchange: Physical Education, K-2. U.C.L.A. Graduate School of Education circa, 1969.

Clein, M. I. and W. J. Stone. "Classification of Educational Objectives: Psychomotor Domain." The Physical Educator. Vol 27, March 1970, 34-35.

Erikson, E. H. Childhood and Society. 2nd rev. ed. New York: Norton, 1963.

Godfrey, B. and M. M. Thompson. Movement Patterns Checklist. Columbia, Mo: Kelly Press, 1966.

Gordon, L. D. Development and Evaluation of Behavioral Objectives for Physical Education Grades K-2. Unpublished doctoral dissertation Columbia, Mo: University of Missouri-Columbia, 1971.

Gordon, L. D., M. M. Thompson, and J. Alspaugh. "The Relative Importance of Various Physical Education Objectives for Grades K-2." Research Quarterly, Vol. 44, No. 2, May 1973, 192-6.

Harrow, Anita J. A Taxonomy of Psychomotor Domain. New York: David McKay Company, Inc. 1972.

Jewett, A., Et. al. "Educational Change Through A Taxonomy for Writing Objectives." Quest, Monograph XV. January, 1971, 32-38.

Keogh, J. F. Developmental Evaluation of Limb Movement Tasks. Technical Report 1-68 (U.S.P.H. S Grant HD 01059) Department of Physical Education. University of California, Los Angeles. December, 1968.

Kephart, N. C. The Slow Learner in the Classroom. Columbus, Ohio: Chas. E. Merrill, 1960.

Krathwohl, D. R., et. al. Taxonomy of Educational Objectives Handbook II: Affective Domain. New York: David McKay, 1964.

Montoye, H. J. (ed.) Introduction to Measurement in Physical Education: Vol. 4, Physical Fitness. Indianapolis, Ind.: Phi Epsilon Kappa, 1970.

Simpson, E. The Classification of Educational Objectives: Psycho-motor Domain. University of Illinois, Research Project No. OE 5-85-104, 1966.

Thompson, M., B. Mann, and M. Dewhirst. Unpublished Materials on Taxonomic Curriculum Planning. Mahomet, Illinois, 1972, 73.

Appendix

A: Sample objectives and learning experiences for selected age groups five through seven.

B: Planning daily lessons for selected age groups five through seven.

C: Sample daily lessons for selected age groups five through seven.

SAMPLE OBJECTIVES AND LEARNING EXPERIENCES FOR EACH OF THE SIX TAXONOMIC CATEGORIES

EARLY CHILDHOOD LEVEL - AGES 5-7

Behavioral Objectives	Learning Experiences
LEARNER WILL OVERTLY DEMONSTRATE:*	
1.10 Knowledges and Understandings of the Human Body	
1.11 Knowledge and Understandings of names and locations of body parts and segments	Play games like "Busy Bee" (touch partner's index finger with your index finger)
1.12 Differentiation among parts of body	Participate in "Hokey Pokey" or "Looby Loo"
1.20 Knowledges and Understandings of Movement Patterns and Skills	
1.21 Understanding of the differences among the various locomotor patterns (walking, running, leaping, jumping, hopping, skipping, galloping)	Teacher sets problem of having children perform a different type locomotor pattern each time signal is given to "change" group responds to identification of patterns used.
1.22 Knowledge and understanding of the movement pattern to use for travelling through different sized spaces.	Set up obstacle course with varying heights and widths, set problem of children exploring most effective pattern for specific space.
1.23 Knowledge and understanding of the changes or modifications in body inclination, length of stride, etc. that are necessary to change	Have children experiment with running at different speeds and for different distances in groups. Discuss changes observed. Can use pictures to illustrate.
1.30 Knowledges and Understandings of Mechanical Principles of Movement	
1.31 Knowledge and understanding of how to control momentum when making a quick stop following a fast run.	Use signal system for children to stop in midst of fast running. Have children explain what helped them stop.

*"Overtly demonstrate" connotes verbal and/or non-verbal communication of the knowledge or understanding.

1.32   Knowledge and understanding of appropriate patterns for various movement requirements. — Play game of "Freeze" (utilizes starting, stopping, balancing, with various locomotor patterns)

1.33   Knowledge of the relationship of leverage to force production in throwing. — Use visuals or verbal description of body and body parts as levers; define lever, force; explore use of arm only, arm and leg opposition, varying lengths of backswing (with and without body rotation).

1.34   Knowledge and understanding of the principles of absorption of force of the oncoming object through increase of time and distance — With bean bags or yarn balls have child explore to accept this principle of increasing time and distance for more effective absorption by joint extension and flexion...pulling arms in toward body as object contacts hands.

1.40   Knowledges and Understandings of Physiologic Factors

1.41   Understanding that rigidity (extreme tension) of body parts makes movement performance more difficult — Have child try to jump with stiff legs (no flexion at knees, hips or ankles), then varying degrees of relaxation which allow flexion

1.42   Understanding that running or jumping rapidly increases the heart rate and the rate of breathing — Have child check own pulse (at neck or wrist), then jump rapidly or run in place rapidly, recheck pulse and note change in breathing (timing not necessary)

1.43   Understanding that one should lift or carry objects that are comparable to own level of strength — Provide objects of varying weights and have children experiment with lifting, pushing or carrying them.

1.50   Knowledges and Understandings of Rules and Strategies

1.51   Understanding that space limitations (boundaries) need to be different for activities which require large movements than for those which require small movements. — Have children select own spaces on the floor; mark own space with a jump rope. Experiment with large movements and small movements of body and body parts and with and without equipment.

Behavioral Objectives   AGES 5-7   Learning Experiences

1.52 Understanding that while differences in distance of a run before take-off in mounting or getting over an object may serve as a deterent as well as an assistance.

Have child try mounting or vaulting objects of varying heights and widths first from a standing position, then vary the lengths of the runs; discuss which runs were beneficial and which detracted from the jumps.

1.53 Understanding that the forward momentum of the body mass combined with the force applied by reaching out to tag a person can produce too much force and make the tagged one fall.

Use a safe object that will fall over or hang a sheet over a rope and have children experiment with touching this with varying amounts of force; gradually increase the distance including a run and touch. Discuss.

1.61 Recognition of different shapes of objects.

Place different object shapes (on large card-stock) on the floor and have child stand at appropriate shaped card (can also use ropes) of name of shapes called.

1.62 Ability to understand and to make simple explanations containing new words, or with different meaning for already known word.

Teacher presents balance problem requiring use of one point and one patch (both words known but not as used in problem presented). Teacher defines (point as one body part supporting the body; patch as one body segment or large surface; seat, back, etc.) Child makes up own balance (different) and tells what he has used.

1.63 Ability to understand the concept of counting by numbers while performing a motoric task.

Provide variety of balls, mats, ropes, as well as free moving space; agree upon total number of times task is to be performed; child performs chosen task, counting aloud.

1.64 Ability to discriminate between even and uneven rhythms.

Teacher: "Can you clap your hands to an even beat? Clap with me; Can you clap your hands to an uneven beat, Clap with me."

1.65 Understanding that energy must be used to do work; that more energy is required as more work is done.

Provide activity which requires children to move slowly then rapidly or to perform a task two or three times, then many times (20?). Compare fatigue level; compare tiring and energy expenditure by having children suggest tasks and discuss differences.

1.66 Understanding that equipment sharing relates to equal use and opportunity.

Provide several (4) stations and different types of equipment (hand apparatus and/or large apparatus). Design, in light of objectives from 4.0, 5.0, and post tasks that may be accomplished. Stipulate that each child must complete at least one task with a specified number (3 or 4) of stations or kinds of equipment. Teacher will signal for change at equal intervals but will not demand that children make change. Allow time to determine degree to which stipulation was met by all; children's feelings about and the role of sharing.

2.10 Appreciation and Acceptance of Physical Activity

2.11 That performance of movement activities is fun and satisfying.

Provide body or object handling tasks (with bean bags, different sized balls, hoops, etc.) which allow child to explore and experiment within his own range of ability without competing with his peers.

2.12 Acceptance of the premise that one feels better (physiologically and emotionally) as a result of participation in movement activities.

Elicit discussion, by children recalling previous instances, of how doing physically active things made them get over anger, feeling "blah," not wanting to do task that had been assigned in another subject.

2.13 Performance in some type of shared movement activity.

Have group hold edges of parachute and move chute up and down synchronously while people exchange positions by going under the

159

Behavioral Objectives

Learning Experiences

chute (all children with red hair; brown shoes; blue shirts)

2.14 Desire to perform movement tasks more proficiently than previously done through increasing the number of times of successful performance of a task.

Provide stations with variety of tasks such as jumping for distance, bouncing a ball consecutively, performing somersaults; inform children that these tasks will be used in group game or activity at later time. Provide card or chart for child to compare his own performance.

2.15 Ability to identify and/or perform movements that express emotions

With children in groups of 3 or 4 have each group decide upon an emotion to portray through movement...different interpretations of same emotion within one group are acceptable. Teacher and/or other groups may try to guess what emotion was being portrayed and make suggestions for other ways to express it.

2.20 Values of Positive Self-Concept

2.21 Recognition and acceptance that if one is unable to touch his toes with his hands without bending his knees that he can by practice increase his flexibility to the point of success.

Provide variety of self-testing activities and/or exercises which indicate improvement in other tasks and/or some which provide opportunity for improvement of flexibility through muscle stretching.

2.22 Recognition that differences in height and/or body size are advantageous as well as disadvantageous in specific activities.

Set up obstacle course (with degree of success based on length of time needed to complete it) and include small, narrow, large, high spaces to go through and under as well as hanging objects to be touched that are placed at varying heights, and large circles (on floor or wall) that are to be covered as completely as possible by one's body.

160

2.23	The ability to follow the directions of the teacher without having to be re-minded.	Teacher instructs children to replace equipment to point at which they got it before moving to the next activity or area. Depending upon success of group may discuss in light of loss of time at new activity, etc.
2.24	The ability to continue to work at a task he needs to improve, rather than reverting to one he already performs well, and seek help if he is ready for the next step.	Have the children form groups of 2-4 in size and have them work individually on tasks (skills) they will need to use in a group activity that is challenging and enjoyable.
2.31	The ability to test his movement performance against a peer in the same light as testing against his own previous performance.	Select a partner of equal ability for combative play (Indian Leg Wrestling, four-square rope pull)
2.32	Recognition of the need to throw an object accurately to his partner if he expects to have a successful game of throw and catch.	Zig-zag shuttle passing with groups of six to eight.
2.33	Recognition and respect of performance limitations of others.	Child leads trio through an assigned series of tasks in a manner allowing others to follow.
2.34	Recognition and respect of values other than familial.	Have child serve as arbitrator in settling play dispute.
2.35	Recognition and respect of contributions of others.	Lummi Sticks-After giving children an adequate repertoire of patterns, have each child create and demonstrate a short pattern for rest of group to duplicate.

2.40 Concepts Regarding Groups

| 2.41 | Realization of Small Group Structures | Partners pick partners for task team activities |

Behavioral Objectives   AGES 5-7   Learning Experiences

2.42   The ability to get along with others
        while working with partners or groups.

        Provide materials as follows: lummi sticks,
        yarn balls, gymnastic equipment, jumping
        ropes, construction paper, scissors,
        crayons, other materials as preferred (may
        have more than 1 set of various materials).

2.421   The ability to accept a decision
        of partner or the group when it
        does not coincide with one's own
        decision.

2.422   The ability to suggest alternate
        ways of solving a movement problem
        that does not appear to be working
        successfully.

        Have class divide into groups of four on
        basis of materials they prefer to work with
        (first come, first serve). Each group
        constructs tasks to be done with provided
        materials and is responsible to teach these
        tasks to other groups.

2.423   The ability to work in a group and
        identify with it on the basis of
        interest in the activity rather than
        on the basis of friendship.

3.10   Agility

3.11   The ability to control one's balance
        at the end of a series of jumps.

        Game of "Magic Square"; or set up lines to
        jump to; or set up boxes into which child
        jumps and balances, etc.

3.12   The ability to change speed and dir-
        ection while moving with a group with-
        out bumping into anyone else.

        Utilizing percussion (drum, handclaps, etc.)
        signals have children run, turn, hop back-
        wards, skip to left, etc. on specified
        signal while keeping one's own space.

3.13   The ability to make rapid changes of
        level without loss of balance.

        Play game of "squat tag" - or have level
        changes made to previously arranged signals.

162

3.20 Balance

3.21 The ability to stand on one foot with the other foot off the floor for a specified length of time.

Perform simple folk dance: "Seven Jumps."

3.22 The ability to utilize the arms and flexion of the joint of legs to maintain balance after a jumping turn.

Include among the tasks at trampoline, from mini--tramp, from elevated area, or from the floor; jumping turns (1/4, 1/2, 3/4, full)

3.30 Coordination

3.31 The ability to visually follow the movements of an object propelled by the hands.

Use tether balls and try by successive hits to wind ball around pole; or suspend a ball (use various sizes) and count number of times can contact ball by hitting it as it swings.

3.32 The ability to visually follow an object rolling toward one and contact it with the foot.

Set tasks at kicking station both for partners rolling ball to each other and on an individual basis kick ball to wall and count number of rebound kicks one can make consecutively.

3.33 The ability to respond immediately by diving into the water when pool edge is touched by teammate.

In groups of 4, set up partner shuttle race across pool and have children time each other from partner's touch to completion of swim to other side.

3.40 Endurance

3.41 The ability to increase the number of times one is able to jump a turning rope over a period of practice times.

At "rope station" provide variety of tasks from: self-turning of small rope, jump the shot, jumping rope turned by others.

3.42 The ability to increase the number of times one can travel the length of the horizontal ladder (or similar equipment) with body weight propelled by hands

At apparatus station such as hanging rope or pole, horizontal bar, parallel bars, climbing apparatus (Lind Climber, Jungle Gym), set up problem experience which will

163

Behavioral Objectives   AGES 5-7   Learning Experiences

elicit hanging and/or travelling, pulling oneself onto or over the equipment, etc.

3.50 Flexibility

3.51 The ability to combine rotation of the head with extension and flexion of the neck.

Utilizing movement exploration, have children discover various movements of the head and neck and compare range of movement.

3.52 The ability to touch the chest to the knees in a tuck position.

Utilize problem such as: How small can you make yourself? Can you make yourself like a ball and roll? Increase flexibility.

3.54 The ability to open and close the fists and to separate the fingers and bring them back together.

Utilize finger play games such as "fly away Jack - fly away Jill."

3.60 Kinesthesis

The ability to resume a previously established position of body and/or body parts without looking.

Have children at stations, set problems of body part positions such as arms raised to particular point; foot lifted 4 inches off floor and have rest of group try to do these and repeat without looking.

3.70 Rhythm

3.71 The ability to perform a locomotor or non-locomotor movement with fluidity.

Select music with even rhythm and uneven rhythm and have children respond and compare ease of achieving fluidity; then without music have them respond to Laban classification of movement (sustained, percussive, etc.)

3.72 The ability to respond to the tempo of a percussive instrument as played by another person.

Using bongo drum, tambourine, or dance drum--at one station or with mass grouping-- have children respond to tempo changes (fast, medium, slow) with hand claps, then with locomotion.

3.80 Strength

Provide station with climbing equipment and have children explore ways to get onto, perform and dismount.

Sufficient arm strength to swing one-self up onto a parallel bar.

3.90 Power

Play "Charlie over the Water" or similar game requiring jumping of specified distances such as modified hop-scotch.

The ability to leap or jump a specified distance by virtue of adequate explosive leg strength.

4.10 Sensori-Motor Abilities

Set up movement problems or utilize stunts: "jumping jack," hop-turns, etc. to elicit unilateral, bilateral and cross-lateral movements.

4.11 The ability to perform unilateral, bilateral, and cross-lateral movements.

Set up obstacle course with vertical and horizontal spacing of varying sizes; play game of "Streets and Alleys" with alleys narrower than streets.

4.12 The ability to select the correct body position (front facing, side facing) for moving between objects placed varying distances apart without overestimating or underestimating the distances.

Set up movement problem for varying size groups which incorporates running, changing direction. Compare moves necessary for different group sizes.

4.13 The ability to run in a group without falling, pushing, or tripping others.

4.14 Discrimination

Assign specific tones (using rhythm instruments) for locomotor and non-locomotor movements. Have children respond to tone with appropriate movement.

4.141 The ability to distinguish auditorily from pre-assigned tonal cues the changes in sound tone.

Behavioral Objectives	Learning Experiences

4.142 The ability to judge the timing needed to side-step an oncoming object when one is in either a stationary or moving position.

In small groups play game of wall-dodgeball, which allows dodger to duck or side-step object thrown at him.

4.143 The ability to move barefooted on various surfaces moving back-wards.

Have barefooted children walk, then run on rubber tire path.

4.144 The ability to judge the arm move-ments made while performing loco-motor activities without watching arms.

Make and identify various size circles with the arms while jumping on the floor or on the trampoline.

4.20 Non-Locomotor Patterns and Skills

The ability to perform a non-locomotor skill that combines arm movements with trunk bending and spinal rotation.

Have children create or imitate movements such as winding up and unwinding a rubber band, being a tree in a windstorm, etc.

4.30 Locomotor Patterns and Skills

4.31 The ability to combine the elements necessary to produce the forward and upward direction necessary to jump over objects.

Include at a "jumping station" such activ-ities as Jump the Shot, jumping a low swinging rope, jump a low height at "high jump."

4.32 The ability to fall in a manner that is not injurious to the performer.

Utilizing a crash pad or tumbling mat, have children experiment with different types of falls, presenting variety in amount of body surface used. Compare; move to falls on floor as individual class members are ready.

4.40 Combining Locomotor and Non-Locomotor Patterns and Skills

The ability to perform a locomotor movement while making body turns on alternate steps (combining locomotor and non-locomotor).

Have children skip and change direction making 1/4 turns on alternate skips; increase turn to 1/2, 3/4, and full turns as individual children are ready.

4.50 Combining Locomotor, Non-Locomotor and Body Awareness

4.51 The ability to perform alternate hopping with trunk bending.

Perform Indian War Dance

4.52 The ability to jump rope while performing a locomotor task.

Have children jump rope while running across gymnasium; can also try on wide walking beam and on trampoline.

4.60 Movement Communication

4.61 The ability to imitate the movements of persons walking on different surfaces or in different media.

Have children name variety of surfaces and media (sand, ice or waxed floor, grass, asphalt; on land, in water, in space) and in small groups explore movements to match the surfaces and media.

4.62 The ability through body movement to indicate fatigue, emotions, vitality.

Utilizing cue cards have children respond by movements which convey: "anger," "happiness," "fear," "bravery," etc.; can use story-play which includes expression of emotions, fatigue and vitality.

4.63 The ability to realize posture/gesture presentation of self, and interpretations of these moods as others see them.

Have the children show their groups how they feel or how they believe they want to feel.

5.10 Sensori-Motor Abilities

5.11 The ability to track and contact a moving object.

At one station provide balls of varying sizes suspended by strings or small ropes and have children hit ball successively as it swings.

Behavioral Objectives   AGES 5-7   Learning Experiences

5.12 The ability to distinguish sounds in near and far space.

Using a variety of percussive instruments (triangle, cymbals, bongo) have group with backs to instrumentation determine the distance from which sound comes.

5.13 The ability to distinguish differences in size and weight of objects.

At an object handling station provide a variety of objects (ping-pong ball, medicine ball, volleyball, softball, etc.). Have children compare sizes and weights; can follow up with identification with eyes closed or blindfolded.

5.14 The ability to determine, without auditory visual or tactile cues, the positioning of body parts.

Play game of "Simon Says" (in small groups) with eyes open and then with eyes closed. Movement calls for each type must be the same.

5.20 Coordination

5.21 The ability to throw different sized objects

Set up throwing stations (rope, volleyball net, wooden screen; each at different heights) with a variety of objects (bean bags, small sponge balls, footballs, etc.). Have child throw object over obstacle to partner. Discuss success/failure causes.

5.22 The ability to kick a ball to a rebounding surface from a specified distance and control the rebound.

Set up a kicking station which has a wall or rebound surface available for a group of 4-6 children. Have a child kick the ball to the wall and stop it in a controlled manner; continue kicks and stops, keeping score of successes.

5.30 Propulsion

5.31 The ability to throw an object so that it hits a specified target.

Set up interesting targets (clown faces with holes for eyes, nose, mouth, etc.) and have

168

children attempt to throw beanbags, then balls, through the holes. Vary distances and kinds of throws.

5.32   The ability to strike (hit or kick) an object with sufficient force that it travels a specified distance (dependent upon size of object and development of child)

Set up groups of 3-4 children using a batting tee. Rotate positions. Place fielders at specified distances, have the batters hit ball to distance of each fielder; can add accuracy of hitting to the fielder when distance is achieved; play modified "tee ball."

5.33   The ability to vary the speed with which one propels an object.

With class divided into small groups (each group provided with variety of objects) have them attempt to throw each object at the same speed. Compare results. With this as springboard throw objects at varying speeds.

5.40   Absorption

The ability to catch a batted ball.

Provide catching station for 3-6 children with a batting tee, soft or plastic ball, and a "fat" plastic bat. Batter tries to direct balls in air and on ground. Fielders try to catch balls. Batter becomes fielder and fielders rotate when ball is caught.

6.10   Coordinated Eye-Hand and Eye-Foot Refinements

6.11   The ability to run and get into position to catch an object one has propelled.

Provide each child in class or at an "object handling station" with a ball. Set tasks of tossing ball in air, bouncing ball on floor and catching it; toss and/or bounce and make complete turn of body and catch.

169

6.12   The ability to move the body into   Children divided into partners or small
        position to contact an object with   groups of 3-4. Have children design a
        the foot.   formation (circle, square, parallel lines)
                                                    and kick ball back and forth; with same
                                                    formation, have groups run or walk in the
                                                    pattern of the formation and kick the ball.

6.20   Coordinated Propulsion of Objects and Locomotion

6.21   With a partner be able to propel and   Divide class into small groups of 4-6. Pro-
        receive an object with the hands while   vide each group with a variety of objects
        running.   (deck tennis rings, balls). Set up relay or
                                                    shuttle relay with partners running from a
                                                    specified line to a specified line and try-
                                                    ing to make as many successful passes as
                                                    possible. Vary the type throw and/or the
                                                    object used.

6.22   With a partner be able to propel and   Same as 6.21 but with kicking pattern.
        receive an object with the feet while
        running.

6.23   To be able to throw (pass) an object   Provide each child in class or at an
        with the appropriate speed (force) to a   "object handling station" with a ball.
        person moving toward the thrower.   Divide group into partners and have them
                                                    experiment with varying amounts of force of
                                                    the throwing and varying degrees of speed
                                                    of the runner. Discuss adjustments
                                                    necessary for success.

6.30   Coordinated Absorption of Objects and Locomotion

6.31   The ability to maintain dynamic balance   Provide a station where children experiment
        while throwing from a run.   with a variety of positions while running
                                                    and passing a football.

170

6.32 The ability to judge the amount of body rotation and joint flexion needed to decrease the force of an object received while one is moving toward the passer.

Provide a station for 6-8 persons, set up partners and do diagonal passing from a specified line to another line or for a specific number of passes with the person receiving the last pass knocking down a pin or throwing to point on wall for score.

PLANNING DAILY LESSONS

In planning daily lessons the teacher will find it helpful to:

1. Plan General Behavioral Objectives utilizing the taxonomic categories and then design specific behavioral objectives for the lesson, and select movement experiences to achieve them.

2. Plan for progression in complexity from first lesson to last lesson within general behavioral objectives categories.

3. Try to plan movement experiences (activities) and methodologies used so that each day each child:

    a. Experiences success and satisfaction

    b. Is challenged

    c. Has maximum participation

    d. Gets some vigorous activity

    e. Understands and accepts lesson objectives for himself

4. Indicate equipment needed and placement in activity area.

5. Indicate methodology to be used per activity per lesson.

6. Include organization of class for various parts of the lesson; utilize illustrations where beneficial.

7. Indicate approximate amount of time per activity per lesson.

8. Include teaching points and possible elaborations on experiences presented.

9. Utilize formal or informal evaluation by students and self of extent to which behavioral objectives were met.

In conducting daily lessons the teacher will find it helpful to:

1. Be firm but friendly.

2. Know the lesson and conduct it in a manner that indicates to the children that he/she enjoys teaching it.

3. Use Teacher Command Method sparingly.

4. Try to anticipate all possible responses of children when utilizing problem solving and be prepared to follow them up with suggestions and/or additional problems.

5. Pay attention to time allotments for parts of lesson, and shift groups accordingly when utilizing stations. If children are not progressing in accordance with plan--be ready for adjustment and briefly inform children of adjustment(s). This will probably require further adjustment for next day's lesson. Do not be a slave to time allotment and at the same time do not let own inattention to time prevent the class from meeting the day's objectives.

6. Plan for scheme of rotation of groups (if utilizing station plan), for changing group formations (parallel lines to squares to circles) that will be the least time consuming and cause least amount of confusion to the children.

7. Utilize color schemes, geometric forms, animal pictures, etc. for quick formation of partners, small groups at beginning of period to avoid waste of time in children selecting partners, etc. Clearly marked stations with task cards (pictures may be used in place of written descriptions) will facilitate achievement of objectives at stations and may also be utilized in allowing children to form groups by selecting station where they desire to begin.

8. Present all parts of lesson in a manner that is clearly understandable to the children. Make certain their understanding of your directions follows your intentions.

9. Keep a record of names of children asked to show their performances, answer questions, be group leaders, etc. so that all children have an opportunity to have positive feelings about themselves and their classmates.

10. Utilize checklists, short memos, etc. to keep record of performance of individual children so that future lessons and/or the specific lesson can be modified.

11. Provide, where appropriate, a means for children to be aware of the extent of their accomplishments without developing a feeling of competition with classmates. The use of series of tasks, elaborations possible, etc. should diminish this possibility.

SAMPLE LESSON PLANS

The following four lesson plans are selected from an ongoing program of elementary school physical education in Champaign, Illinois. They were selected as examples of progression in meeting specific objectives (sample lessons 1 and 2), variety in methodology, (lessons 2,3,4), variety in activity and meeting several different behavioral objectives (all lessons). All lesson plans incorporated meet the suggestions for daily lesson planning listed previously.

SAMPLE LESSON 1 (Grades 1-2)

Taxonomic Categories: 1.64, 2.32, 2.42, 3.31, 3.72, 4.141.

Specific Behavioral Objectives

Learner shall demonstrate the ability to:

1. Distinguish (by clapping, and moving the body) the difference between even and uneven rhythms

2. Move an object to an imposed rhythm

3. Cooperate in large group activities

Equipment

Rhythm sticks--2 per child

and

Instruments

Parachute

Methodology

Teacher Directed

Time	Procedure	Formation	Teaching Hints
5-10 minutes	I. Introductory Activity A. Can you clap your hands to an <u>even</u> beat? 1-2-3-4 etc. All clap in unison B. What kind of beat am I clapping? 1. Clap uneven 1+a 2+a 3+a 2. Can you clap this <u>uneven</u> beat with me? Clap in unison C. Clap word rhythms D. Move around the gym to even and uneven beats. Listen and move Teacher changes beat	Sitting in center of gym own space	May need to explain beat, uneven, and even to grades 1 or 2. Use phrases to get meaning across-- <u>Even</u> "clapping is steady" "Every clap is like the one before it" <u>Uneven</u> "sounds like a horse when he gallops" "Long-short, long-short" Clap (Teacher) <u>1+a 2+a 3+a</u> Pick children's names and clap them. *For interest rhythm sticks could be used by children rather than clapping--or even and uneven rhythms could be repeated using sticks and moving around gym.

Time	Procedure	Formation	Teaching Hints
10 min- utes	II. Parachute Activi- ties A. Walk around cir- cle (all children holding to para- chute) Is this an even or uneven beat? B. Skip around--de- cide whether it is even or uneven C. hop--even or un- even D. All together-make the parachute move up and down to an even beat- then uneven beat	Back to cen- ter circle formation	II. Count beats when needed.
10 min- utes	III. Making Rhythms Pass out rhythm instruments 1. shakers 2. sand-paper 3. bells 4. sticks Call out 1 of 4 instruments make an even or uneven rhythm under para- chute.		Teacher calls out type of rhythms--children hurry under--do rhythm and return to their original positions.

SAMPLE LESSON 2 (Grades 1 and 2)

Taxonomic Categories: 2.23, 2.24, 2.32, 3.32, 3.41, 4.141.

<table>
<tr><th>Specific Behavioral Objectives</th><th>Equipment</th></tr>
</table>

The student will demonstrate the ability to:

1. Respond to externally imposed rhythm by marching to music, responding to words of a song, and rope jumping

2. Coordinate eye-foot locomotion in rope jumping

3. Increase physical endurance through constant activity

4. Listen and follow directions

Equipment

Record Player

Marching Record

3 or 4 long jumping ropes

Methodology

I, II--Teacher Directed

III--Task

Time	Procedure	Formation	Teaching Hints
5-10 min-utes	I. Warm-up A. Perform own in-terpretation of marching any-where in gym. B. Marching in for-mation	Own space Straight line Split	Self-directed Teacher directed
5 min-utes	II. Rhythm and Body Awareness Development Looby-Loo Song Game Chorus: Child-ren do locomotor pattern around circle, hands joined	II. Circle facing one another	See pg. 238-239 Latchaw Games and Rhythms Teacher join in game and be leader if necessary.

177

Time	Procedure	Formation	Teaching Hints
15 min-utes	Verse: As each verse is sung, children act out words III. Rope Jumping A. Build the Castle—Children "jump" by put-ting weight on hands and jump-ing feet over rope B. Build the Castle with regular jump—if rope gets too high duck under without touching it. C. Blue Bells—jump rope which is mov-ing in half swings D. Jump full turning rope E. Jump to Rhymes children may know IV. Collect equipment	In small groups	Child holding on rope end, assistant holding other, change child holding end often Some may be able to do cartwheel over rope—encourage stretching legs into the air. Encourage all to try Change rope speed ac-cording to ability For problems cue "jump" "jump" Make experience suc-cessful Children help

SAMPLE LESSON 3 (Grades 1-2)

Taxonomic Categories: 1.33, 1.34, 2.23, 2.32, 2.42, 3.11,
                        4.142, 5.30, 5.41.

Specific Behavioral Objectives

Learner shall demonstrate the
ability to:

1. Stop and start quickly

2. Create body movements from a
   visual stimuli

3. Follow directions, work alone,
   and work with others

4. Recognize and pronounce spelling words

5. Propel a ball

6. Absorb force by
   catching balls

Equipment

Shoe string

Familiar spelling words
on cards

Different size and shape
balls--one per child

Methodology

I, II, III, Teacher Directed

IV Problem Solving: Ex-
ploration

Time	Procedure	Formation	Teaching Hints

5 min.	I. Warm-up
	  A. Run and Freeze on Signal
	  B. Stop and stretch various body parts
		Own Space	Vary run to other locomotor patterns
			Stretch neck, arms, legs in air and on ground, weight on hands and stretch

5 min.	II. Imagery/creative movement Follow the Shoe-string--Be like it.	Own Space	Wiggle, tangle, wad, stretch, fold, and swing the shoestring--children should follow.
10 min.	III. Low Organized Game combining spelling with Physical Development "Come Along"	Sit for Explana-tion.	Explain simply demon-strating with child-ren as explanation takes place.

179

Time	Procedure	Formation	Teaching Hints
	All stand with right hand out of circle and facing clockwise. One child outside circle is tagger.	Circle	
	Teacher presents spelling word (example: w-h-o)		Start with short words
			When children understand game go to longer words which will involve many people. Make two circles.
	Tagger goes around circle and tags a <u>w</u>, w tags <u>h</u> and h tags an <u>o</u> then original tagger says the word and begins to run to open space in the circle left by the children who represent the letters of the word. The one left without a space becomes the new tagger		Correct and add rules after game is underway.
			Make sure words are familiar.
			Repeat till all children have played in each circle.
10 min.	IV. Ball Handling	Own Space	Let them experiment with propelling ball.
	A. Free Play		
	B. Guided Play through Questioning		"Can You?" Bounce with one hand
			Bounce and walk
			Bounce and run
			Change hands, etc
	V. Pick Up Equipment		Children Help.

SAMPLE LESSON 4 (Grades 1-2)

Taxonomic Categories: 1.30, 2.32, 2.42, 3.21, 3.80, 4.52.

Specific Behavioral Objectives	Equipment
Body Handling: The student will demonstrate the ability to:	Balance Beam
	Mini-tramp
1. Maintain balance in various body positions, on varying height, while supported and while un-supported.	Swedish box
	Mats
2. Coordinate body movements in gymnastics and tumbling skills	Four marking pencils of different colors
3. Propel and absorb his body weight (on to and off of large apparatus)	**Methodology**
	I. Teacher Directed
4. Work in small groups	II. Task; Exploration

Time	Procedure	Formation	Teaching Hints
5 min.	I. Warm-Up A. Flexibility Curling-stretch-ing-bridges B. Absorption and propulsion of force: Jump, fall, and roll.	Own Space	Color code the children Go through simple loosening-up exercises. Review hide nose, elbows and knees, land on soft large body part and keep rolling.
5-7 min. at each sta-tion. Ro-tate clock-wise	II. Gymnastics Stations A. Beams (Children experiment with low and medium beams): 1. loco-motor patterns forward, back-ward, side, 2. Balances on body parts on beam 3. Turns. 4. Changes of levels	Class equally divided in four stations	Have children try activities at each station by themselves first, then with a partner.

181

Time	Procedure	Formation	Teaching Hints
	B. Box (Swedish Box)		As children create different ways of performing at each station, have others try to duplicate.
	Children experiment with:		
	1. Variety of ways to get on to and over the box.		
	2. Variety of things they can do on the box.		
	3. Variety of ways to get off box.		
	C. Tumbling-Individual, Partner, or Group stunts and tumbling. (rolls, animal walks, balances).		Stress principles of body handling in comments to children as they perform.
	D. Mini-tramp, Experiment with:		
	1. Achieving two foot land on bed of mini-tramp.		
	2. Achieving soft, controlled landing.		
	3. Incorporate turns		
	4. Perform stunt after landing that helps absorb body momentum		